Taliesin West

At Home with Frank Lloyd Wright

Nora Burba Trulsson
Principal photography by Andrew Pielage
Foreword by Stuart Graff

In Association with the Frank Lloyd Wright Foundation

Rizzoli
New York

New York Paris London Milan

Contents

A Midway Gardens sprite, an artistic collaboration between Frank Lloyd Wright and Alfonso Ianelli, guards the exterior of the Garden Room and a grassy courtyard.

FOLLOWING SPREAD: The entry sequence to Taliesin West guides visitors past the Office on the left and the Drafting Studio on the right. Wright's use of desert masonry in buildings and garden walls links the structures to the site.

Taliesin West's Pergola is the site of many outdoor dinner events.

Foreword

Frank Lloyd Wright's Taliesin West is more than the historic home and studio of one of the world's greatest architects; it is a living testament to the power of great design to change the way we interact with nature, with the arts, and with each other. Conceived in 1937 as a winter camp to offer respite for seventy-one-year-old Wright, his family, and his Fellowship of apprentices, Taliesin West soon became a source of inspiration for Wright's work. It was a place where his principles of design, inspired by nature's forms and processes, were tested to see whether they could produce works of genius in the same way that the verdant landscapes of his native Wisconsin produced the work that made his reputation. Wright's ideas passed that test—and the period from 1937 to his death in 1959 represented an extraordinary advance in both his creativity and productivity.

Yet it's not enough to look at Taliesin West through only the lens of its architecture, or even the landscapes from which it was born and into which it is integrated. Taliesin West was, and remains, its people, because there's no great architecture unless it serves the lives of those who inhabit it. In Wright's words, "Man takes a positive hand in creation whenever he puts a building upon the earth beneath the sun. If he has any birthright at all, it must consist in this, that he, too, is no less a feature of the landscape than the rocks, trees, bears or bees of that nature to which he owes his being."

In Nora Burba Trulsson's exploration of the site and the stories of those who built, worked, lived, and celebrated here, we begin to see why Taliesin West still inspires people to connect more deeply with the world around them. Our visitors often tell us that the place "feels different" from other places—more serene, a part of the world and not merely in it. As someone who for a time lived as part of the Fellowship, Nora has a unique ability to convey how that felt and what it meant to live with that feeling day to day. That's why I asked her to write this book, weaving together stories of lives and architecture.

Frank Lloyd Wright was well-read and fond of quoting (and even revising) the work of his favorite authors. I don't know whether Wright ever read E. M. Forster—his works are not referenced by Wright—but I think he might find meaning in an oft-quoted passage from *Howard's End*: "Only connect!...Only connect the prose and the passion, and both will be exalted, and human love will be seen at its height. Live in fragments no longer." Wright and the Fellowship accomplished that at Taliesin West, and it's why the work that we still do today at the property continues to resonate with relevance.

STUART GRAFF
President and CEO, Frank Lloyd Wright Foundation
Taliesin West, January 2024

Introduction

Taliesin West was and remains more than a collection of groundbreaking buildings designed by its most famous resident, architect Frank Lloyd Wright. It was a community, a place where seventy-some people lived, studied, and worked, inspired to follow the philosophy of organic architecture and a life filled with art and beauty as espoused by Wright and his wife Olgivanna.

The community members, known as the Taliesin Fellowship, were part of an architectural training program, formed by the Wrights in 1932, for younger apprentices and senior members of the Fellowship as a way to keep Wright's architectural practice in gear. Over the next decades, more than a thousand members cycled through the program, all willing to not only learn about architecture and art, but to migrate seasonally between the Wrights' two properties, the original Taliesin in Spring Green, Wisconsin, and Taliesin West, established in 1937 in the desert of what is now Scottsdale, Arizona. "Taliesin" (pronounced Tally-ESS-in), which means "shining brow" in Welsh, reflected Wright's intention to create buildings that were "of the site," not on it. Taliesin West's location at the base of the McDowell Mountains epitomized that intention and had a spiritual appeal to all who experienced the high desert setting above the lights of Phoenix. Some stayed for a year, some more, moving on to work and life beyond the arid, cactus-strewn setting. Still others stayed for a lifetime.

PREVIOUS SPREAD: A night view of the Drafting Studio on the left and the original dining room to the right. The second story includes guest apartments.

OPPOSITE: Taliesin West's acreage at the base of the McDowell Mountains is lush with desert vegetation that provides a habitat for animals such as deer.

BELOW: Frank Lloyd Wright and client Rose Pauson, to his left, discuss her Phoenix home in the desert.

Lifelong friendships were formed here. First loves, flings, and marriages took root in the desert. Young people came to terms with their sexuality here. Affairs, breakups, betrayals, intrigues, power plays, and divorces occurred. Children were born, raised, left, and, sometimes, came back to Taliesin West. Deaths were also part of the cycle.

There was work, both architectural and the day-to-day projects needed to maintain Taliesin West's many buildings and its several hundred acres. Young apprentices learned not only to draft and design, but also how to cook for dozens, keep plumbing systems flowing, repair crumbling desert masonry walls, build new additions, and keep the landscape trimmed. The making of music and art was encouraged. If you played an instrument or sang, you were in the orchestra or chorus. Painting and sculpting, also encouraged.

Dinners happened here, parties, skits, performances, concerts, holiday festivals, teas, birthday celebrations, cocktail hours, weddings, baby showers, and funerals. Taliesin West offered a full life, a sense of family, a community.

It was, in other words, a place many called home.

Taliesin West may have been conceived as a rustic desert camp, but Frank Lloyd Wright enjoyed luxuries such as this roadster, with Olgivanna Wright at the wheel. The car was one of many Wright vehicles painted a signature Cherokee Red hue.

Frank Lloyd Wright in the Drafting Studio.

OPPOSITE, CLOCKWISE FROM TOP LEFT: Olgivanna and daughter Iovanna Wright enjoy a desert picnic with their dogs. Fellowship members outside the Office. Olgivanna in the Taliesin West desert, abloom with spring poppies. A tea gathering on the Sunset Terrace.

FOLLOWING SPREAD: A circa-1930s image of Taliesin West's desert site, with rocks in the foreground destined for desert masonry walls.

Origins

When Frank Lloyd Wright and Olgivanna Wright first set foot on the property that would become Taliesin West in 1937, the Sonoran Desert stretched out for miles before them. Reachable only by rutted roads that undulated through washes and past stands of saguaros, the site was some twenty-five miles from downtown Phoenix and fifteen miles from Scottsdale, then a sleepy, unincorporated community. Backing up to the McDowell Mountains, the area was sparsely populated, save for cattle ranchers and shepherds who passed through with their flocks, migrating to and from seasonal pastures. The hillsides were dotted with boulders bearing petroglyphs, evidence of the ancient Sonoran people, who lived in the desert scrub centuries earlier. To the northeast lay Fort McDowell, a late-nineteenth-century military post.

Despite the remote locale, the architect and his wife were smitten—"the top of the world!" Wright exclaimed. In December of that year, they acquired several hundred acres of government land, at a reported $3.50 per acre. Wright immediately sent a telegram from Arizona to the Taliesin Fellowship in Wisconsin that read: "Weather warm beautiful site in hand. Come...soon...bring shovels rakes hoes also hose. Eighteen drawing boards and tools...viola cello rugs...and whatever else we need." Two months later, construction began on Wright's new desert camp, his laboratory for modern architecture.

OPPOSITE: Frank Lloyd Wright, in the foreground, supervises the replanting of a saguaro cactus by a group of early apprentices.

BELOW: Young apprentices help with a construction project in the 1980s.

FOLLOWING SPREAD: A rendering of San Marcos in the Desert, an unbuilt hotel project that brought Wright to the Arizona desert in the 1920s.

The Wrights were not strangers to Arizona's sunshine, dry air, and otherworldly landscape. Wright first came to Phoenix in 1927 as a consulting architect for the building of the Arizona Biltmore hotel. There, Wright met Alexander J. Chandler, a veterinarian, land developer, and founder of the city of Chandler, southeast of Phoenix. Dr. Chandler envisioned another luxurious resort, San Marcos in the Desert, to be built near Chandler on the slopes of South Mountain. Working on the project with his draftsmen Wright also supervised the construction in 1929 of a desert camp on the site, dubbed "Ocotilla"—a misspelling of ocotillo, the thorny desert plant—where the group could work and live. The camp, made up of angular tent structures built of canvas and wood, served as a prototype for the design of Taliesin West several years later. The stock market crash led Dr. Chandler to abandon the resort project, and Wright to abandon the camp.

Back at his home and studio in Spring Green, Wright and Olgivanna faced dwindling commissions and a large property to maintain during the Depression. In 1932, they conceived the idea of the Taliesin Fellowship, the establishment of Wright's architectural apprentice program, in which young students interested in architecture would pay tuition and handle daily maintenance of the Wisconsin property in exchange for soaking up knowledge at the side of the master architect.

A long bout of pneumonia and the bitter cold of yet another Wisconsin winter drove Wright and Olgivanna back to Arizona during that winter of 1937, where they stayed at the genteel Jokake Inn at the base of Camelback Mountain near Scottsdale. It was there that the two decided that the desert needed to be their winter home and acquired the land near the McDowell Mountains.

By February of 1938, some thirty members of the Fellowship began what would be annual migrations between Taliesin in Wisconsin and what was named Taliesin West in Arizona. The young crew arrived ready for adventure and construction, sleeping bags and tools in hand. It was an arduous undertaking; winter rains drenched the members of the Fellowship and created raging rivers out of dry desert washes, while strong winds blew apart the early makeshift shelters. Carving out roads and excavating the site for buildings proved difficult due to the preponderance of caliche, the concrete-like layer of calcium carbonate found in desert soil. And there were the neighbors—rattlesnakes, scorpions, tarantulas, javelinas, and even the occasional mountain lion known to lurk in the McDowells.

But the magic of the desert prevailed for the Wrights and the apprentices. A full moon and a sky filled with stars, hillsides covered in golden poppies and deep blue lupines in spring, beaming sunshine that turned pale Wisconsin dwellers ruddy after a few months. The buildings began to rise.

Wright designed the camp to reflect the desert, with angled walls and rooflines that mimicked the forms of the mountains, details inspired by the spikes and ridges of cactus, and floor plans that encouraged the Fellowship to spend as much time outdoors as in. Using brown butcher paper, Wright sketched out Taliesin West's core. The first structure completed was a vault, to keep architectural drawings safe from rains, wildfires, and gnawing creatures. It was built of desert masonry, walls made with stones found on site, and a dry concrete mix placed into wooden forms, setting the vocabulary for the rest of the buildings, which used redwood beams and canvas as the roof material. Wright's office, the drafting studio, kitchen, and the original dining room were the next to be completed. As the Fellowship returned each year, more structures rose from the desert floor, including the Wrights' private quarters, and the Kiva, Cabaret, and Pavilion Theatres.

Early scenes from the 1930s and 1940s showcase Taliesin West's construction and camp-like lifestyle. In the upper left image, Olgivanna Wright's brother, known as Uncle Vlado, cleans a shotgun he was known to wield to keep trespassers at bay.

In the late 1940s, Wright's desert utopia was rattled when the federal government installed a vast line of power poles just past the Taliesin West property, spoiling the once-pristine view. Wright contacted President Harry Truman, insisting that the power lines be buried, to no avail. After threatening to pull the plug on his desert home and decamp to southern Arizona, Wright cooled down, redesigning the approach to Taliesin West to turn its back to the structures, emphasizing mountain views instead.

At first, living quarters for the members of the Fellowship were primitive. After sleeping bags on the ground and lean-tos, the next step was a sleeping box, elevated from the desert floor. Eventually, the property was dotted with sturdy canvas tents, an idea borrowed from the shepherds who passed by the McDowells. The first year, Taliesin West had no water and electricity only by generator. A weekly trip to the YMCA in downtown Phoenix provided showers, while water for cooking was hauled in, thanks to a friendly rancher nearby. Kerosene lanterns provided nighttime illumination. By the 1940s, the Apprentice Court was completed—luxe accommodations compared to tents—which originally provided fourteen rooms for men and women, with toilet and shower facilities. A guest deck was added above the kitchen and loggia to accommodate visitors, and, over the years, more rooms were added for younger apprentices. Some of the senior members of the Fellowship began constructing their own private homes and cottages on Taliesin West land, away from the central core. Others built elaborate shelters, graduating from the simple canvas tents.

As in Wisconsin, daily life for the Fellowship was that of a vibrant arts community, filled with periods of creativity in architecture, music, and fine arts, interspersed with chores, including construction, cooking, cleaning, gardening, and more. For many years, Taliesin West was a self-contained culture, hard to reach by visitors in the remote desert hills, but as roads improved and the Wrights became enmeshed in the local community, social and public events dotted the Taliesin West calendar.

After Wright's death in 1959 and Olgivanna's passing in 1985, construction and expansion continued at Taliesin West, with additional living quarters added, as well as a bookstore, student lounge, and an archive building. Wright's architectural practice continued as Taliesin Architects in both Arizona and Wisconsin until 2003 when it was disbanded, and the apprenticeship program evolved into a traditional architectural school, which became a separate entity and moved to a new location in 2020.

Today, Taliesin West and Taliesin in Wisconsin are owned by the Frank Lloyd Wright Foundation, and the emphasis is on preservation of the buildings and stewardship of Wright's creative legacy. Taliesin West was designated a National Historic Landmark in 1982 and a UNESCO World Heritage site in 2019, as part of eight Wright-designed projects in the

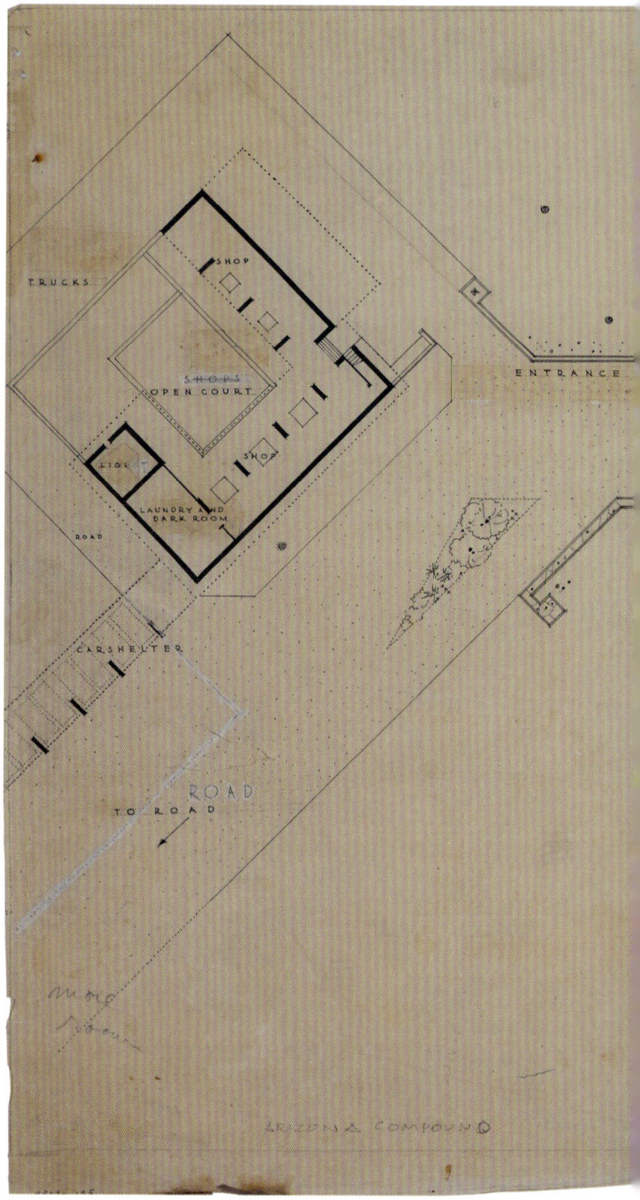

An original plan of Taliesin West, including a workshop at upper left and the Wrights' quarters and the apprentice apartments on the right.

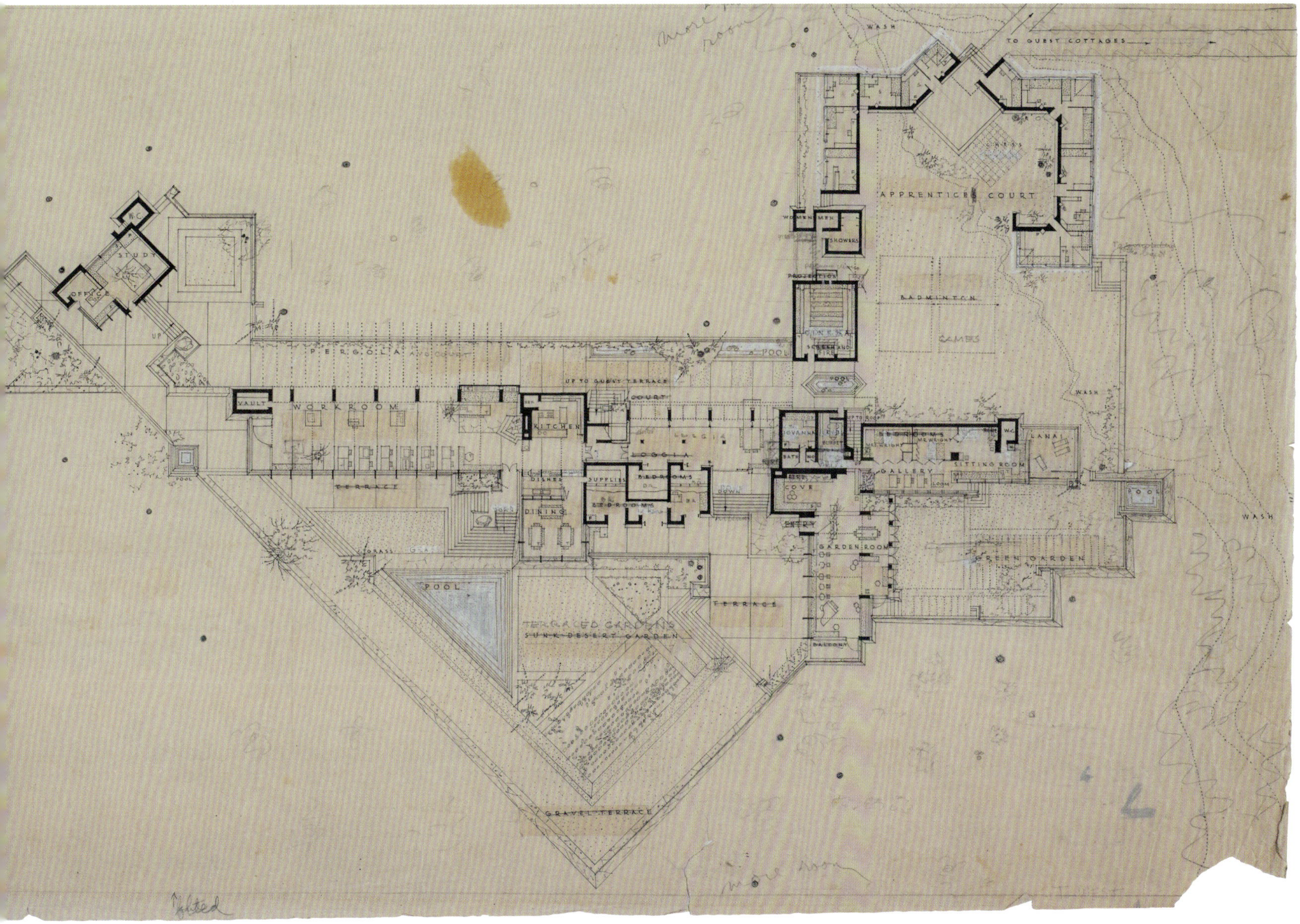

United States. While few Fellowship members still live on site, more than 100,000 visitors come to the desert site annually, which, more than ever before, is open to the public with educational, cultural, tourism, and social opportunities.

Rising from the desert, construction of Taliesin West's main core begins in the late 1930s, with shapes and rooflines echoing the nearby McDowell Mountains. The breezeway and Sunset Terrace are to the right.

CLOCKWISE FROM FAR LEFT: The exterior of the Sun Trap (later called the Sun Cottage), the Wrights' first living quarters. The inside of the Sun Trap, now used as guest housing. A water tower and a shallow pool mark the walkway between the Kiva, a small theater on the left, and the Wrights' private quarters on the right.

Exterior and interior views of the Sun Trap, originally built for the Wrights.

An early view of the walkway between the Kiva Theatre (on the left) and the Wrights' private quarters.

OPPOSITE: Taliesin West, at one with the desert.

Garden Room

On a Saturday evening in spring, members of the Fellowship walk through a low, red-painted door and into the Garden Room. Dressed in tuxedos and gowns, they sip gin and tonics or scotch on the rocks, help pass gold-hued platters of cheddar cheese and crackers, and mingle with a dozen or so invited guests. Younger apprentices, sometimes awkwardly tugging at bow ties and smoothing satin dresses, are gently discouraged from congregating in a corner and encouraged to learn the fine art of small talk and polite listening. The start of a musical interlude—piano and violin—hushes the crowd. After forty-five minutes of cocktails, guests and the Fellowship members stream out in the desert night, headed for dinner.

The ritual of cocktails that, for decades, marked the start of formal evenings, always began in the Garden Room—also known as the Living Room—which was long revered by members of the Fellowship as a gathering place. It's where weddings and wakes took place, Christmas caroling and design critiques. Initially, it was used as the Wrights' "parlor," where they could spend quiet family evenings or invite special guests for tea. It was an unspoken rule that members of the Fellowship entered only by invitation or during Saturday evening cocktails. After the Wrights' passing, the room evolved into a community gathering spot, an egalitarian space where all members of the Fellowship had access.

OPPOSITE: The Garden Room, most recently restored to its 1950s iteration.

BELOW: Frank Lloyd Wright and Olgivanna Wright enjoy tea by the hearth.

Construction on the Garden Room began in the winter of 1939–1940, adjacent to the Wrights' private quarters and a landscaped courtyard on one side and the Sunset Terrace on the other. The room was designed with a roof that slopes up to the east and includes a long, built-in banquette and a line of low windows that elongate the space. When seated, guests see the Wrights' private garden and the tops of nearby mountains. To one side, an alcove seemingly spills out into the garden. Originally, the roof, supported by sloped redwood beams, was canvas. Like a tent, the room was open to desert breezes, sealed off when necessary by canvas flaps lowered by a series of pulleys. Eventually, the roof was replaced with fiberglass panels, and, later, acrylic panels, and the canvas-flap openings were enclosed with glass. A fireplace was added later, and a terrace was enclosed.

While the Wrights entered from their private quarters, guests to the Garden Room came in through the red door and made three turns in a low-ceilinged foyer before entering the voluminous space.

Views of the Garden Room, likely in the late 1940s before its expansion.

Olgivanna Wright works on a project in the Garden Room.

Wright's piano and, for many years, his daughter Iovanna's harp graced the room. Wright designed an origami-like armchair for the setting, several of which provided seating, along with apprentice-made hassocks and store-bought upholstered armchairs and ottomans. Wright's beloved Asian ceramics and Native American pots were arranged around the room, as were sheepskin throws as a decorative touch. Over the years, other artworks, were added—hand-painted screens by Fellowship members Davy Davison and Gene Masselink, a bronze bust of Wright by artist and Fellowship member Heloise Christa, and two mosaics by writer, politician, and ambassador Clare Boothe Luce, who, along with her husband, *Time* magazine publisher Henry Luce, were frequent guests of the Wrights.

In the early years, the Garden Room was the Wrights' private domain, where they spent quiet evenings reading or playing music, with Wright at the piano and Iovanna on harp.

Wright would pore over his collection of Japanese woodblock prints on a large table specially designed for the artworks. Private teas and cocktail receptions were held there when the Wrights entertained potential clients or luminaries, such as actor Charles Laughton and poet Carl Sandburg, who were passing through Arizona. While the room seemed to encourage elegance, scholarly pursuits, and quiet conversation, Wright was known to occasionally pound out not a Beethoven piano concerto, but rather a boogie-woogie tune on the piano—likely met by an Olgivanna eye roll.

During cocktails before formal evenings, Wright and Olgivanna often sat in the origami chairs with one of Olgivanna's dogs at their feet while guests greeted them. In addition to the Luces, the Wrights were keen on inviting notable guests and clients for these evenings. Solomon Guggenheim and Edgar J. Kaufmann, who commissioned Wright's most notable works, mingled there. Actress Anne Baxter, Wright's granddaughter, came often. The who's who of Phoenix society were invited. In later decades J. Carter Brown of the National Gallery of Art and Walter Cronkite sipped cocktails in the space. For years, Fellowship members, including architects Kamal Amin and, later, Arnold Roy, served as bartenders, fixing drinks in a small anteroom behind the Garden Room.

During the Christmas season, apprentices put up a tree in the Garden Room. They were also charged with cleaning the space, not to mention wrangling the occasional snake that might slither along the banquette. Christmas caroling and gift exchanges occurred, organized by Olgivanna. During Easter, the Taliesin chorus, made up of members of the Fellowship,

Frank Lloyd Wright contemplates Japanese prints, while daughter Iovanna's harp creates a stately backdrop. Fellowship members decorate the Garden Room's Christmas tree in the 1990s.

Olgivanna Wright sits in one of the Garden Room's origami chairs. The pendant light fixture behind her mimics the form of Taliesin West's tent shelters.

CLOCKWISE FROM ABOVE: A young apprentice catches some sleep during one of the Saturday formal evenings. The Wrights entertain guests. Olgivanna confers with textile designer Dorothy Liebes, who worked on several projects for Wright. The Wrights host a meeting over tea.

A hand-painted screen by Fellowship member Davy Davison graces a corner of the Garden Room and depicts an aerial abstraction of Taliesin West.

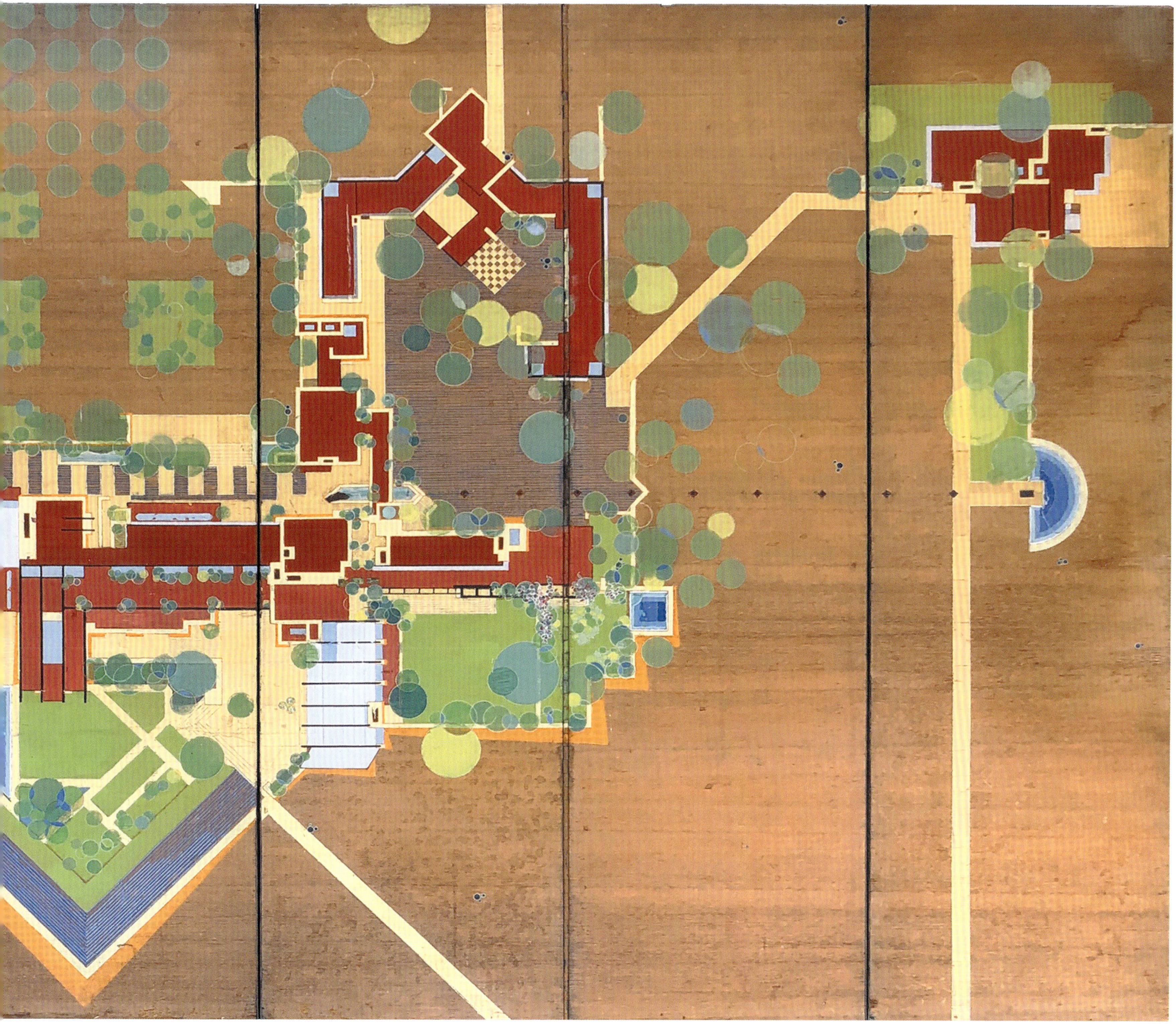

Benches and chairs of Wright's design, built by members of the Fellowship, provide seating in the Garden Room.

performed to a small audience before outside guests arrived. The student Box Projects, in which young apprentices created architectural or artistic works for review, took place in the space, with Wright critiquing the presentations and projects. After Wright's death, Olgivanna and architect William Wesley Peters and other senior members of the Fellowship continued the critiques. Wright also gathered the Fellowship in the Garden Room on Sundays after breakfast for talks, touching on topics such as architecture, art, and politics. In later years, Olgivanna continued the tradition, but she also incorporated practical matters and philosophical topics, usually based on her studies with spiritualist and teacher George Gurdjieff.

As the years progressed, the Garden Room served as a backdrop for significant life events. Peters married Svetlana Alliluyeva, Josef Stalin's daughter, at Taliesin West in 1970, with a reception hosted in the Garden Room. (Peters had been married to Wright's stepdaughter, also named Svetlana, who died in a car crash with their two-year-old son in 1946.) After Wright's death at a Phoenix hospital in 1959, his wake was held in the room, where, dressed in a white suit and resting in a coffin built by apprentices, his body remained until it was driven to Wisconsin for burial. Upon Olgivanna's passing in 1985, she, too, lay in repose in the Garden Room, dressed in a beloved blue Pucci dress. For years after her death, Olgivanna's birthday was marked with a breakfast of blinis served in the Garden Room, a nod to her Slavic roots.

By the late 1980s, as the Fellowship found its footing without the Wrights, the Garden Room still functioned as the venue for formal evenings, but, during the day, it served as a site for more practical events, such as weekly Fellowship meetings. Once the apprentice program transitioned into an accredited school, students also held meetings in the room. As they received their master's degrees in architecture, many students were feted with graduation ceremonies in the space, open to family and friends. The Garden Room also served as the location for informal parties, music performances, and skits.

By the 1990s, tours of Taliesin West became more formalized, and visitors came through the room, learning about the architecture and other details from tour guides. As in the Wrights' era, visits by notables were not uncommon. Architect Michael Graves contemplated Wright's work as he sat in one of the Garden Room's origami chairs. Margaret Thatcher visited with her husband, lingering in the space. Celebrities such as Sean Connery, Barbra Streisand, and Candice Bergen were captivated by the room's edited views and natural light.

Today, the room has been updated with modern comforts including heating and air conditioning, and restored to its 1950s design, when both Wrights used the space as their own.

FOLLOWING SPREAD: A large table in the Garden Room displays Wright's collection of Native American pottery and Asian ceramics. Wright's piano still occupies a corner of the room.

Kitchen

At six thirty on a Wednesday evening, an apron-wearing apprentice walks over to a series of cables next to the kitchen's walk-in cooler, ringing the adjacent tower's bells to announce dinner. Within a few minutes, apprentices, senior members of the Fellowship, and a handful of employees and guests filter past the kitchen's butcher block island and into the dining room, where they are served dinner—beef stroganoff, perhaps, with a vegetable and a salad—on melamine plates. To drink? Water poured from a large pitcher set on each table.

The heart of Taliesin West, the Kitchen is a utilitarian space made elegant through the use of a two-story volume that captures natural light. The glass doors lead to the Dining Room. BELOW: As seen from the second-story guest deck walkway, the kitchen was always a hub of activity.

Mealtime at Taliesin West was a community event, and the kitchen served as the hub, the heartbeat of the community. For decades, kitchen duty was a week-long task for both apprentices and senior Fellowship members, a responsibility relished and perfected by some, and loathed and avoided by others. It required military precision and planning to serve three meals, plus morning and afternoon teas, to a community of seventy-some people—a community that included a large percentage of young people with prodigious appetites—that swelled to ninety or more during the weekly formal evenings.

Food fueled Taliesin West's construction projects, work in the studio, arts programs, and more, so a functioning kitchen was one of the first structures to be built, replacing a temporary lean-to erected in a desert wash the first year the Fellowship found themselves in Arizona. Built in 1938, the kitchen was placed by Wright at the center of the growing desert complex, connecting the drafting studio, the original indoor dining room, and a loggia that was eventually enclosed to create the current larger dining space.

Though utilitarian, the kitchen was designed to be architecturally striking: a two-story volume, illuminated by windows from the upper-level terrace and marked by redwood siding and red concrete flooring. Originally, a walk-in cooler, a windowless vegetable storage room, and a pantry kept food supplies at the cooks' fingertips. As the years went by, the kitchen was monitored by county health inspectors, necessitating the addition of commercial refrigerators, a freezer, vent hoods, and sanitary dishwashing equipment.

For many years, a neatly typed work list prepared by senior Fellowship member Kay Rattenbury was tacked to the kitchen's bulletin board on Sunday night, outlining Fellowship work duties, which included tasks such as construction, sanitation, shopping, and getting the mail, in addition to cooking chores. The male senior Fellowship members were assigned to breakfast preparations so, in theory, they could spend the rest of the day in the drafting studio working on income-producing projects—something that might smack of sexism today. The lunch and dinner cook was often another senior Fellowship member or an apprentice with culinary skills. They were aided by one or two kitchen assistants—often new apprentices who learned timing and organization, not to mention how to chop vegetables and scrub pots. There was also usually a tea cook, who would prepare cookies or light snacks for morning and afternoon breaks. The Wrights had their own small kitchen where their weekday meals were prepared for them to eat in their private quarters.

The week's cook put together a suggested menu for lunch and dinner, which was scrutinized, updated, and approved by Olgivanna, Rattenbury, or Minerva Montooth, another senior Fellowship member. Menu inspiration came from heritage, tradition, culinary trends, and three-ring binders stuffed with recipes for tried-and-true dishes.

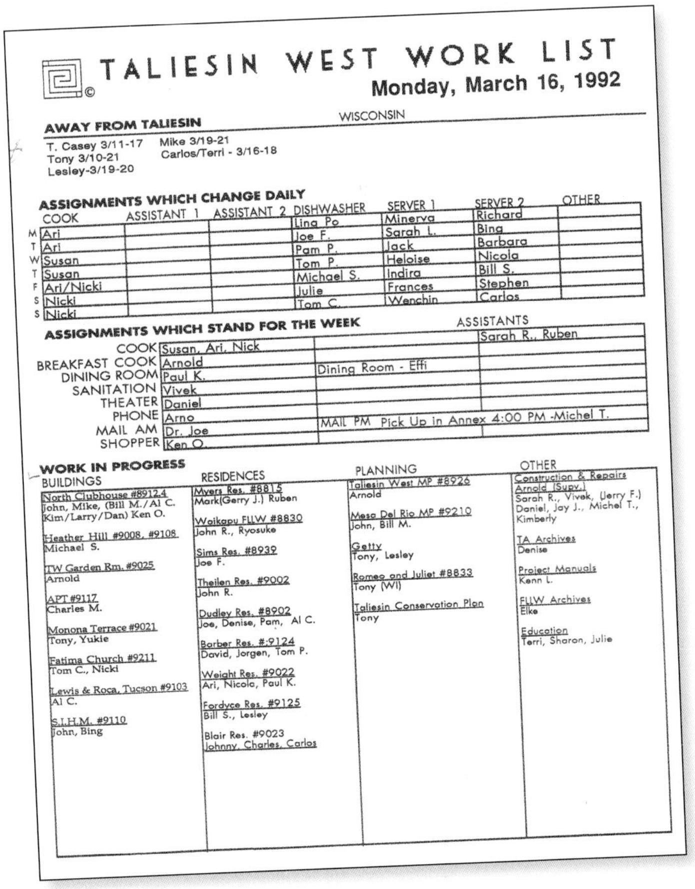

TALIESIN WEST WORK LIST ©

Monday, March 16, 1992

WISCONSIN

AWAY FROM TALIESIN

T. Casey 3/11-17 Mike 3/19-21
Tony 3/10-21 Carlos/Terri - 3/16-18
Lesley-3/19-20

ASSIGNMENTS WHICH CHANGE DAILY

	COOK	ASSISTANT 1	ASSISTANT 2	DISHWASHER	SERVER 1	SERVER 2	OTHER
M	Ari			Lina Po	Minerva	Richard	
T	Ari			Joe F.	Sarah L.	Bing	
W	Susan			Pam P.	Jack	Barbara	
T	Susan			Tom P.	Heloise	Nicola	
F	Ari/Nicki			Michael S.	Indira	Bill S.	
S	Nicki			Julie	Frances	Stephen	
S	Nicki			Tom C.	Wenchin	Carlos	

ASSIGNMENTS WHICH STAND FOR THE WEEK

			ASSISTANTS
COOK	Susan, Ari, Nick		Sarah R., Ruben
BREAKFAST COOK	Arnold		
DINING ROOM	Paul K.	Dining Room - Effi	
SANITATION	Vivek		
THEATER	Daniel		
PHONE	Arno		
MAIL AM	Dr. Joe	MAIL PM Pick Up in Annex 4:00 PM -Michel T.	
SHOPPER	Ken O.		

WORK IN PROGRESS

BUILDINGS	RESIDENCES	PLANNING	OTHER
North Clubhouse #8912.4 John, Mike, (Bill M./Al C. Kim/Larry/Dan) Ken O.	Myers Res. #8815 Mark(Gerry J.) Ruben	Taliesin West MP #8926 Arnold	Construction & Repairs Arnold (Supv.) Sarah R., Vivek, (Jerry F.) Daniel, Jay J., Michel T., Kimberly
Heather Hill #9008, #9108 Michael S.	Waikapu FLLW #8830 John R., Ryosuke	Mesa Del Rio MP #9210 John, Bill M.	TA Archives Denise
TW Garden Rm. #9025 Arnold	Sims Res. #8939 Joe F.	Getty Tony, Lesley	Project Manuals Kenn L.
APT #9117 Charles M.	Theilen Res. #9002 John R.	Romeo and Juliet #8833 Tony (WI)	FLLW Archives Elke
Monona Terrace #9021 Tony, Yukie	Dudley Res. #8902 Joe, Denise, Pam, Al C.	Taliesin Conservation Plan Tony	Education Terri, Sharon, Julie
Fatima Church #9211 Tom C., Nicki	Barber Res. #:9124 David, Jorgen, Tom P.		
Lewis & Roca, Tucson #9103 Al C.	Weight Res. #9022 Ari, Nicola, Paul K.		
S.I.H.M. #9110 John, Bing	Fordyce Res. #9125 Bill S., Lesley		
	Blair Res. #9023 Johnny, Charles, Carlos		

A weekly work list was posted on the kitchen's corkboard every Sunday, outlining duties for apprentices and senior Fellowship members.

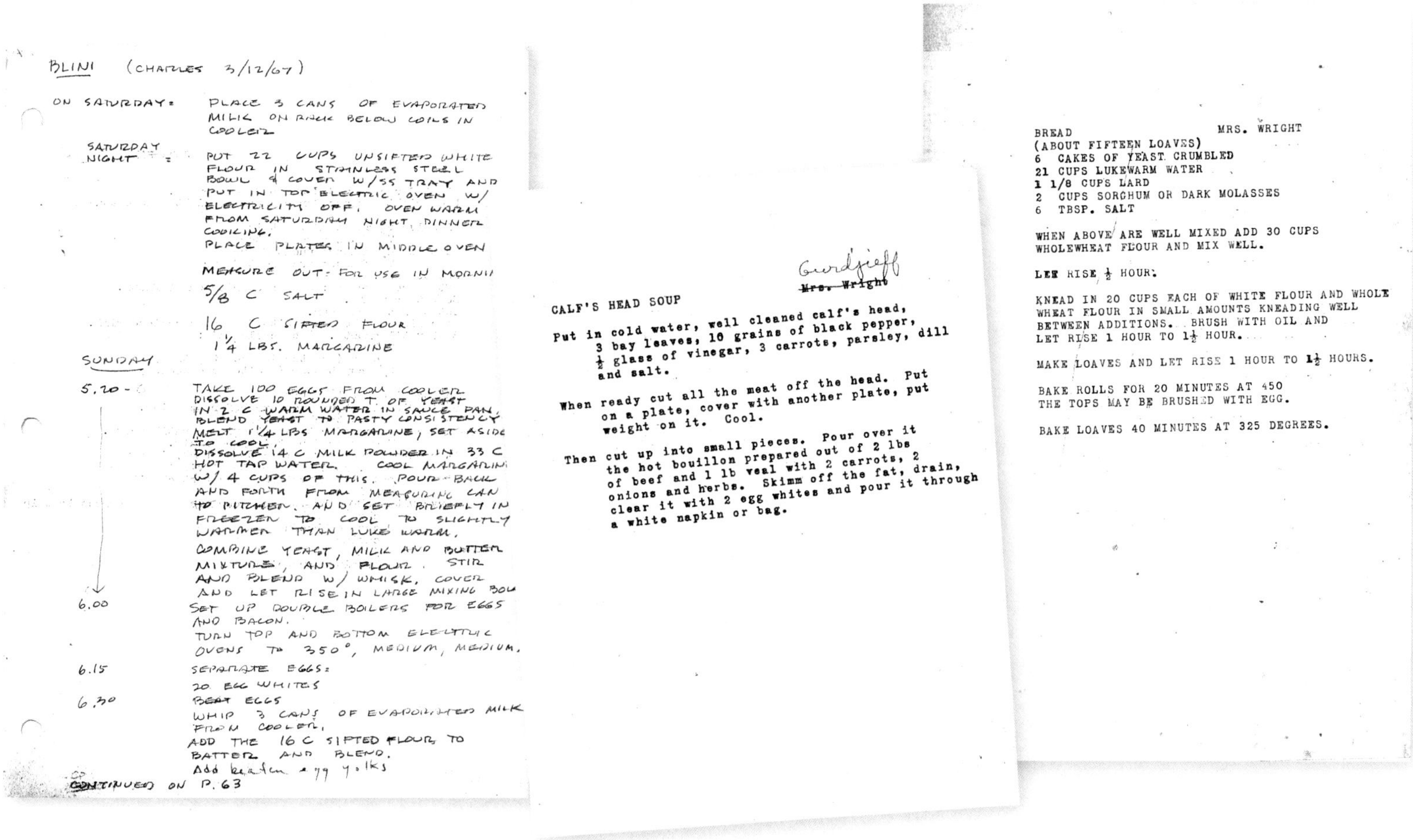

BLINI (CHARLES 3/12/67)

ON SATURDAY: PLACE 3 CANS OF EVAPORATED MILK ON RACK BELOW COILS IN COOLER

SATURDAY NIGHT = PUT 22 CUPS UNSIFTED WHITE FLOUR IN STAINLESS STEEL BOWL & COVER W/SS TRAY AND PUT IN TOP ELECTRIC OVEN W/ ELECTRICITY OFF. OVEN WARM FROM SATURDAY NIGHT DINNER COOKING.
PLACE PLATES IN MIDDLE OVEN

MEASURE OUT: FOR USE IN MORNI[NG]
5/8 C SALT
16 C SIFTED FLOUR
1 1/4 LBS. MARGARINE

SUNDAY

5.20 – TAKE 100 EGGS FROM COOLER
DISSOLVE 10 ROUNDED T. OF YEAST IN 2 C WARM WATER IN SAUCE PAN, BLEND ~~YEAST~~ TO PASTY CONSISTENCY
MELT 1 1/4 LBS MARGARINE, SET ASIDE TO COOL.
DISSOLVE 14 C MILK POWDER IN 33 C HOT TAP WATER. COOL MARGARIN[E] W/ 4 CUPS OF THIS. POUR BACK AND FORTH FROM MEASURING CAN TO PITCHER. AND SET BRIEFLY IN FREEZER TO COOL TO SLIGHTLY WARMER THAN LUKE WARM.
COMBINE YEAST, MILK AND BUTTER MIXTURE, AND FLOUR. STIR AND BLEND W/ WHISK, COVER AND LET RISE IN LARGE MIXING BOW[L]

6.00 SET UP DOUBLE BOILERS FOR EGGS AND BACON.
TURN TOP AND BOTTOM ELECTRIC OVENS TO 350°, MEDIUM, MEDIUM.

6.15 SEPARATE EGGS:
20 EGG WHITES

6.30 BEAT EGGS
WHIP 3 CANS OF EVAPORATED MILK FROM COOLER.
ADD THE 16 C SIFTED FLOUR TO BATTER AND BLEND.
Add beaten egg yolks

CONTINUED ON P. 63

Gurdjieff ~~Mrs. Wright~~

CALF'S HEAD SOUP

Put in cold water, well cleaned calf's head, 3 bay leaves, 10 grains of black pepper, ½ glass of vinegar, 3 carrots, parsley, dill and salt.

When ready cut all the meat off the head. Put on a plate, cover with another plate, put weight on it. Cool.

Then cut up into small pieces. Pour over it the hot bouillon prepared out of 2 lbs of beef and 1 lb veal with 2 carrots, 2 onions and herbs. Skimm off the fat, drain, clear it with 2 egg whites and pour it through a white napkin or bag.

BREAD MRS. WRIGHT
(ABOUT FIFTEEN LOAVES)
6 CAKES OF YEAST CRUMBLED
21 CUPS LUKEWARM WATER
1 1/8 CUPS LARD
2 CUPS SORGHUM OR DARK MOLASSES
6 TBSP. SALT

WHEN ABOVE ARE WELL MIXED ADD 30 CUPS WHOLEWHEAT FLOUR AND MIX WELL.

LET RISE ½ HOUR.

KNEAD IN 20 CUPS EACH OF WHITE FLOUR AND WHOLE WHEAT FLOUR IN SMALL AMOUNTS KNEADING WELL BETWEEN ADDITIONS. BRUSH WITH OIL AND LET RISE 1 HOUR TO 1½ HOUR.

MAKE LOAVES AND LET RISE 1 HOUR TO 1½ HOURS.

BAKE ROLLS FOR 20 MINUTES AT 450
THE TOPS MAY BE BRUSHED WITH EGG.

BAKE LOAVES 40 MINUTES AT 325 DEGREES.

A kitchen binder held a variety of Taliesin West recipes, including those for blini, bread, and calf's head soup, said to cure Frank Lloyd Wright of his pneumonia.

While Taliesin in Wisconsin had abundant vegetable gardens that supplied ingredients, at Taliesin West, rabbits, javelina, and deer decimated attempts at growing produce. Although a citrus orchard provided grapefruit, oranges, and lemons, other fruits and vegetables came from the canned bounty of Taliesin's Wisconsin garden, Phoenix farmer's markets, or other suppliers.

Olgivanna guided the original recipes, reflecting her Slavic heritage, which included borscht, blini, kasha, and zrazi, a stuffed beef dish. During the Depression years and the shortages of World War II, parsnips were sometimes the entrée, as were calf's head soup and roasted squirrel, with bewildering instructions to cook a young squirrel for two hours, and an older one for three hours. How a rodent's age was determined is still a mystery. During the 1950s through the '70s, Fellowship travels to New York and Europe introduced chicken divan, curries, and Irish lamb stew to the repertoire, reflecting the group's growing culinary sophistication.

OPPOSITE: Above the kitchen, the bell tower signaled meal times.

William Wesley Peters, at left, leads a kitchen crew project. BELOW: The week's cook was in charge of the menu and did most of the cooking, with the help of several apprentices.

By the 1980s and '90s, Mexican dinners and sushi nights became fixtures. As more international apprentices joined the Fellowship, the menus began taking on a global tone: Swedish meatballs, Middle Eastern shawarma, Greek spanakopita, and German sauerbraten began making appearances. The dishes served most often? Chicken Arlington, baked with a soy sauce and honey glaze; and chili, served for lunch on Saturdays with cornbread and cottage cheese.

Desserts were important, and also reflected a blend of eras and cultures, with sweets like raspberry kissel, prune soufflé topped with zabaglione, Black Forest torte, spice cake, and strudels rounding out a meal. The weekly cook was also responsible for baking more than a dozen loaves of the rustic, whole wheat and molasses "Taliesin bread," served with all meals.

Special occasions were celebrated by Taliesin West's culinary team. Long after the Wrights had passed, their birthdays (Olgivanna's in December, Wright's in June) were still marked by the serving of their favorite cakes. At Easter, in addition to hundreds of eggs boiled prior to dyeing and making paska, a sweet cheese, baking baba was a group event. Per Olgivanna's Orthodox upbringing, the traditional Slavic sweet bread was baked in tubes made of brown butcher's paper. Before the advent of the kitchen's industrial mixer, the men of the Fellowship worked out their aggressions by punching the yeasty dough, while women stood by with butter knives to scrape extra dough off their fingers and wipe sweat from their brows (again, a scenario not likely to be repeated in today's culture). After the breads were baked, community members cooled the towering loaves by rolling them on pillows, so they wouldn't collapse and could be served intact to several hundred Easter breakfast guests. During formal evenings, the main cook had to make sure the food was lugged from the main kitchen, without spilling or sloshing, to be plated in the Cabaret Theatre's small catering kitchen. Whether a special occasion or weekday meal, plating and presentation were important, the kitchen crew learned. Meals had to look attractive, and every plate needed to be colorful and appealing.

Working intensely side by side in the kitchen for a week was a learning experience for apprentices and senior Fellowship members alike, and not without some drama and shenanigans. On Sundays, the cook was supposed to empty the cooler and serve leftovers for lunch, leaving a clean slate for the next week. Woe to the cook who left behind expired mystery foods wrapped in foil. Cooks who used every pot, pan, and utensil were openly reviled by the kitchen help forced to scrub, and re-scrub, the kitchenware. Occasional mishaps forced the kitchen crew to pivot and innovate. One cook ambled into the pantry before a shift, only to find his main ingredient missing and presumably consumed by hungry apprentices. He put together rice, water chestnuts, and celery to create a quasi-Chinese dish that was liked by all. A week in the kitchen was physically and mentally stressful—one apprentice reported an average seven-pound weight loss each week he worked—and the previous week's kitchen crew traditionally had Mondays free of work duties to recuperate. For some, the walk-in cooler, with its virtually soundproof walls, proved to be a good place to let loose a tension-releasing primal scream.

Apprentices and senior Fellowship members learned to cook for a crowd, which numbered up to ninety people during the Saturday evening formal dinners.

Coca-Cola

Sometimes, Fellowship members steered clear of the kitchen's culinary offerings. When word got out that certain cooks who lacked skills were in charge of the week's meals, arrangements were made by some to eat in town or, for those lucky enough to have a private kitchen, cook something on their own. Ditto for certain dishes—liver and onions, for example, a divisive entrée that drove some to avoid dinner. Seasonings sometimes also ignited squabbles between diners and kitchen crew, particularly if something was deemed over- or under-salted. When Olgivanna oversaw the kitchen, she was merciless if a dish was not up to her exacting standards. But when a meal was a hit and second helpings were requested, praise from Olgivanna and the Fellowship was generous and rewarding for the kitchen crew.

By the 1990s and early 2000s, meals became more informal during the week, served buffet-style on the kitchen's butcher block island. As the apprenticeship program evolved into an accredited architecture degree program, it was decided that students needed to study and not spend as much time in the kitchen. Professional chefs, with varying degrees of tempestuousness, took over the kitchen duties, with apprentices and senior Fellowship members stepping in for special occasions.

Today, the kitchen is used by groups attending the Taliesin Institute programs, caterers for private events, and for other activities at Taliesin West.

The kitchen was often the site of after-meal shenanigans. LEFT: Baking babas, a traditional Easter bread, was a group effort. Through trial and error, the Fellowship learned to cool the freshly baked bread on pillows so they would not lose their shape.

Dining Room

At dinner one night in Taliesin West's Dining Room, a senior member of the Fellowship and an apprentice sat at a table with their architectural clients, a couple in the process of building a custom home. Not long into the meal, all four detected movement along the room's desert masonry wall. There, poised to pounce on any après-dinner crumbs, was a desert pack rat, skittering along the wall's V-shaped groove. Though the rodent moment was met with slight alarm by the clients, the architect and apprentice shrugged their shoulders—it was dinner and a show. Like other spaces at Taliesin, the Dining Room balanced civilization and the nature of the surrounding Sonoran Desert.

Also known as the Fellowship Dining Room, the room was once a north-facing loggia off the kitchen, built as part of the site's core in the late 1930s with the original, smaller dining space positioned south of the kitchen. The loggia, dotted with picnic tables, was where occasional alfresco meals were eaten, chess matches occurred, and, in the 1940s when weaving became a popular preoccupation for some of the Fellowship, looms were set up, protected from sun and rain by the deep overhang.

After World War II, the Fellowship outgrew the original dining area, and the loggia was glassed in to create the new dining space, which was expanded several years later to accommodate some fifty diners. The room included a closet and nook to one side—possibly designed for a children's table and later used as the blueprint room—as well as a band of cabinetry along one wall. Wood-topped tables that could seat four and metal-framed chairs, patterned after Frank Lloyd Wright's Midway Gardens design, were crafted on-site by members of the Fellowship. The glass walls, with mitered corners, afforded views of the McDowell Mountains and the Taliesin West citrus grove. Movable glass panels and a pivoting red door leading to the breezeway allowed for airflow.

As part of the weekly work schedules at Taliesin West, one apprentice was assigned to the Dining Room, responsible for setting up the space and keeping it clean. Creativity was encouraged—apprentices could place the tables individually, push several together, or line them up in a row.

They were also in charge of flower arrangements for each table, often a challenge since there usually wasn't a budget for store-bought posies. Instead, the desert and, later, cultivated gardens yielded blooms and objects—and lessons in floral design. Red pyracantha berries were okay, but bougainvillea bracts wilted quickly. Prickly cholla cactus branches, though artistically displayed, were a painful disaster.

The Dining Room was where the Fellowship had everyday meals, and where some festive events were enjoyed. Tables and chairs were built on site and could easily be rearranged to suit the occasion.

As the Dining Room was typically used by Fellowship members and sometimes staff, everyone had a unique napkin ring for their cloth napkins, which were laundered weekly. Unless one landed in a plateful of tomato sauce, the napkins were placed back in the rings and stacked on a sideboard for use at the next meal. Despite some grumbling about the loss of decorum, paper napkins eventually replaced cloth to save on laundry bills.

Those who set up the room often displayed their artistic approaches. Some plopped tables, chairs, flowers haphazardly. Others used the space as a creative laboratory to test interior design skills—one apprentice set up the chairs around tables at forty-five-degree angles to create a unique pattern, while another made paper flowers for the tables when the desert yielded no inspiration. In the early days, rainstorms wreaked havoc on the original roof, so pots and pans from the kitchen dotted the Dining Room, catching the drips and leaks, adding an unintentionally rustic touch. The apprentice in charge of maintaining the Dining Room's appearance could expect a scolding from senior Fellowship if something was off, such as water in the flower vases not being changed often enough or crumbs being left on the floor. And woe unto anyone who used the blueprint machine in the dining nook and forgot to close the door during meals, allowing noxious ammonia fumes to waft across the tables.

Like a high school cafeteria, there was a bit of social structure during meals in the Dining Room. The Wrights didn't take many meals in the Dining Room, usually eating in their private quarters. Newer apprentices often tried to sidle up to senior Fellowship members, particularly architects they admired. Being late to a meal sometimes meant having to take the last seat next to someone you might not enjoy as a dining companion. Some senior Fellowship members started with cocktails with others in private quarters, then had a merry group to occupy a larger table. Until sometime in the early 1980s, the Fellowship's children ate early—and separately from their parents—under the watchful eye of the "weekly

OPPOSITE: Decorated here for a special event, the original dining room eventually proved to be too small for the growing Fellowship. The adjacent loggia was enclosed to create the current larger Dining Room, and the old space became a meeting room. LEFT: Fellowship member and architect John Rattenbury gives a speech in the Dining Room. TOP: The Dining Room served as a staging area for the dyeing of Easter eggs. MIDDLE: Smaller Fellowship celebrations, such as birthdays, anniversaries, and retirements were often held in the Dining Room.

mother," a woman assigned to take care of the young ones while the parents worked in the studio, office, or elsewhere.

Though the somewhat intimate space was designed for Fellowship and some staff, there was often room to accommodate a handful of guests, usually architectural clients. Not knowing that Wright had imposed a ban on saltshakers on the tables, one guest asked for salt and was met by startled silence. Some guests who shared meals were famous. After a tour of Taliesin West, singer Art Garfunkel, of the Grammy-winning duo Simon & Garfunkel, was invited for lunch with the Fellowship and explained the origins of their hit song "So Long, Frank Lloyd Wright." Garfunkel, who'd studied architecture, asked collaborator Paul Simon to write a song about the architect. Instead, Simon used the words enigmatically to signal his desire to dissolve the duo.

In addition to daily meals, the Dining Room served other purposes. Just off the kitchen, it served as a prep room for the Easter celebration, where flower arrangements were made, eggs dyed, and goose eggs—once used as party favors for guests—were artistically hand-painted by senior Fellowship members, including William Wesley Peters, Ling Po, and Cornelia Brierly. There were meetings, graduation parties, baby showers, and birthday fetes. Each June 8, the members of the Fellowship who did not decamp to Wisconsin celebrated Wright's birthday in Arizona by setting a place for him and serving his favorite cake—sponge cake layered with strawberry jam, chopped walnuts, whipped cream, and chocolate drizzle. Once, in honor of Fellowship member and artist Heloise Crista's birthday, apprentices struck poses from her figurative sculptures in the Dining Room. With many apprentices going home for the holidays, the remaining Fellowship members would gather in the Dining Room for a festive Thanksgiving or Christmas meal, with the space decorated to the hilt.

On Sunday mornings after breakfast, Wright and, later, Olgivanna, gave philosophical talks in the Dining Room or nearby Garden Room. While worshipping at church was never explicitly forbidden, the Sunday morning talks were a subtle way of keeping members of the Fellowship on campus, so to speak, and away from outside influences.

The Sunday talks took on a reverential atmosphere, but skits were the opposite. Olgivanna was particularly fond of the humorous, short plays, which often gently skewered someone or a project the group was involved in. Wigs, costumes, and makeup were employed, and even those without theatrical talent were encouraged to participate. Often taking place in the Dining Room after a meal, the skits were a stress-reducing interlude between architectural projects, and construction, maintenance, and other duties at Taliesin West.

Today, the Dining Room looks much the same as it did when it was first enclosed. It is still used for staff meals, meetings, gatherings, and special events, and as a gallery space for art exhibitions.

LEFT: A view of the kitchen's bell tower and, in the foreground, the loggia with picnic tables, which was later enclosed to create the present Dining Room. BELOW: The Wrights' private dining area had a view of the garden.

Drafting Studio

At four thirty in the morning, one bleary-eyed apprentice shuffles into the Drafting Studio, hoping to catch a few quiet hours to work on an architectural project before the breakfast bell rings at six thirty. After an hour or so, he's joined by several architects—senior members of the Fellowship—also looking for a jump-start on work. By seven thirty or eight, the airy, capacious studio is filled with some thirty architects, apprentices, and support staff, and the steady buzz of conversations is punctuated by ringing phones. The energy continues all day and, often, well past midnight to meet deadlines. The only time the studio seems still is between one and two in the afternoon, when most Fellowship members disappear for a traditional post-lunch siesta.

If the Kitchen was Taliesin West's heart, the Drafting Studio was its over-caffeinated brain, an architectural beehive from which gems of architecture emerged. Frank Lloyd Wright designed it as the centerpiece of his desert site, and Fellowship members built it, largely by hand, in the winter of 1938–1939. Grounded in desert masonry walls, the studio's roof—originally crafted with redwood beams and canvas—angles north toward the mountains. Before glass and doors were added, the studio was tent-like, with canvas flaps covering some of the sides. Warmed by a large fireplace at its eastern side, the studio is anchored on the west by a stone vault, where Wright stored his drawings to be safe from fire, water, and desert creatures. To the south, the studio overlooks a shallow, triangular pool, which, before glass was installed, cooled desert breezes as they wafted indoors.

The studio's hand-built drafting tables were placed in neat rows, accommodating the architects and apprentices. In the early days, Wright had his table closest to the fireplace, and the architects faced him with their tables in a row overlooking the pool. Apprentices were assigned drafting tables in the middle of the space. The closer to Wright, the better, a hierarchy that continued well after his death, when apprentices jockeyed to be closest to the architect with the most projects. Once tours of Taliesin West became more formalized in the 1980s, apprentices who sat closest to the windows overlooking the pergola learned to focus on work as docent-led tours went by.

To keep things neat, and to protect drawings from inevitable ceiling leaks during rainstorms, each table had red oilcloth that unrolled to cover drawings, T-squares, pencils, and more at the end of the workday.

The Drafting Studio's roofline angles north, capturing views of mountains and, closer by, the bougainvillea-filled Pergola. The hand-built drafting tables include rolled-up oilcloth covers. Below: Frank Lloyd Wright checks work in progress.

In the early years before many of the other structures were built, the studio also served as a multipurpose room. Wright had a grand piano placed at one end of the space, and the Fellowship had after-hours chorus rehearsals there. Wright and Olgivanna often dined in the studio, while Fellowship members used it as a de facto lounge, gathering spot, and sleeping quarters, if rain, scorpions, or howling coyotes drove some out of their tents.

As he did with other spaces, Wright would often rework the studio seasonally, tinkering with the beam structure, adding glass, changing details. At some point early on, he had the scored concrete floor painted his signature red, ensuring an annual maintenance headache that continued for decades. Young apprentices were charged with completing the project at night in the empty studio, artfully painting around tables and file cabinets until the wee hours, so the floor would dry by morning.

Artist Ling Po confers with Wright on a project in the early 1950s. The artist collaborated with the architect on renderings of many notable buildings. ABOVE: An early view of a corner of the Drafting Studio before it was enclosed with glass and a more permanent roof structure.

Traditionally, apprentices were not assigned to the studio at first. Instead, they were put on construction duty to learn how buildings were put together, expanding the camp and, in later years, working on renovations and restorations. When they were finally assigned to a table, their first tasks were to trace existing drawings, over and over again, often under the watchful eye of Ling Po, the Fellowship's architectural rendering artist. Only when the apprentices mastered the rendering skills required were they given more architectural tasks in the studio, slowly climbing the design ladder. All were expected to follow decorum in the studio. While both men and women were not expected to wear business attire given the desert setting, they were expected to behave professionally. Once the Wrights' private living quarters were finished, Olgivanna rarely made appearances in the studio. But when she did, often with one of her large dogs in tow, apprentices and architects stood, as a sign of respect.

Under Wright, the apprentices had a front row seat to projects conceived in the last two decades of his life, including New York's Guggenheim Museum, Price Tower in Oklahoma, and numerous Usonian homes. When Wright passed away in 1959, he still had numerous projects in progress, leading to the formation of Taliesin Associated Architects (later shortened to Taliesin Architects) as the continuation of his practice. Wright's son-in-law and first apprentice, William Wesley Peters, took over as chief architect. Under his leadership, unbuilt Wright designs were completed, including Gammage Auditorium, a performing arts hall at Arizona State University; a private home; and the First Christian Church, all in the metropolitan Phoenix area. In California, the Marin County Civic Center was another major Wright design.

OPPOSITE: Senior Fellowship member and architect John Rattenbury and apprentices in the late 1980s. A photograph of Wright keeps watch over the Drafting Studio. LEFT: Wright's son-in-law William Wesley Peters became Taliesin's chief architect after Wright's death in 1959. BELOW: Peters supervises the Drafting Studio in the early 1950s.

Far from merely finishing Wright's work, Taliesin Architects continued with a sizable body of work, including the Pearl Palace and Damavand College in Iran, a signature music building for Arizona State University—designed to complement the adjacent Gammage Auditorium—and renovations and additions for the Arizona Biltmore resort, the project that first brought Wright to the state. After Peters died in 1991, John Rattenbury became chief architect, and work continued at a breakneck pace, with custom homes, golf clubhouses, and, in Madison, Wisconsin, the signature Monona Terrace Convention and Community Center, based on a 1938 design by Wright, finally built in 1997.

By the late 1980s, the Drafting Studio, while vibrant with work, became a bit more relaxed. Apprentices wore headphones to listen to music while drafting and a handful of their dogs became fixtures, lolling in the shade under the adjacent pergola or occasionally coming in to cool off on the concrete floor.

The biggest revolution in the studio came with computers and the advent of CAD (computer-aided design) technology. In the late 1980s, long before most firms acquired them, Taliesin West's studio was dotted with monitors, gifted by Mike Riddle, one of the originators of the AutoCAD system. Along with his newly developed software, FastCAD, Riddle, who was in a relationship with one of the members of the Fellowship, taught architects and apprentices the program, thus putting one of the country's most historic architectural practices at the cutting edge of technology. But the computer age had a few hiccups for Taliesin Architects. Besides a learning curve to leave behind vellum and pens, some of the senior members had issues with aesthetics—the monitors ruined the studio's clean lines. A solution, for several years, was to encase the monitors in attractive wood cupboards that sat atop the drafting tables.

Along with computers, other changes came the studio. Wright's apprenticeship tradition was transformed into an accredited program, morphing into the Frank Lloyd Wright School of Architecture and offering a master's degree in architecture. (It split from the Frank Lloyd Wright Foundation and its quarters at Taliesin and Taliesin West and relocated elsewhere in 2020.) As such, the apprentices began spending more time with formalized studies. With a heavy workload, the architecture firm started hiring outside architects and support, as well as offering internships through other universities. Briefly, Taliesin Architects had a satellite office in Phoenix. While the migration back and forth to Wisconsin still went on, by the late

An early view of the Drafting Studio, when shade structures allowed for working outdoors.

Desert masonry walls and steps link the Drafting Studio to its desert site. A boulder marked with petroglyphs serves as sculpture near the studio's back door. ABOVE: Angled beams echo the forms of the nearby mountains. The solid volume at the right end of the studio is the vault, completed in the 1930s as a fireproof storage room for architectural drawings.

1980s, so much of the architectural work was in the western United States that many of the Fellowship's architects opted to stay in Arizona all year long.

By 2003, Taliesin Architects disbanded, brought forth by dwindling projects and the aging of the senior members of the Fellowship, many of whom had learned architecture and design at the side of Wright. The closure of the practice also marked the end of the Fellowship, one of the longest-lived intentional communities in American history. Wright's apprentice program and his architectural practice produced hundreds of successful architects and designers. While some stayed for a lifetime, many went off and had successful careers and practices elsewhere, including such internationally known architects as John Lautner, E. Faye Jones, and Paolo Soleri.

Today, the Drafting Studio is animated with programs developed by the Taliesin Institute, hands-on learning experiences for architecture and design students, professionals, and lifelong learners. The studio also hosts school groups and camps, exhibitions, and other events.

A vintage exterior view and a more recent interior view of the Drafting Studio, in the computer era. Painting the signature red hue on the concrete floor was an annual maintenance project for apprentices.

FOLLOWING TWO SPREADS: By night, the Drafting Studio's north-facing red doors have a dramatic appeal. Viewed from the south at dusk, the Drafting Studio glows like a lantern.

Office

Anyone who walked into Taliesin West's office in the 1970s or '80s would have been in the midst of a beehive of activities. Four or five Fellowship members with administrative skills had small desks jammed amidst boxes and file cabinets, while Dick Carney, Wright's one-time secretary who became the business manager and CEO, juggled and delegated everything from prospective apprentice applications and paying bills to greeting VIP visitors and processing requisitions for everything from nails and lumber to tortillas and enchilada sauce. Phones rang constantly and, in warmer months, air conditioning units, jerry-rigged into one of the glass doors—before the advent of a central HVAC system—hummed in the background.

It was a decidedly different ambiance when the space was constructed as Frank Lloyd Wright's private office between 1938 and 1939, one of the first buildings to rise from Taliesin West's desert site. Though Wright had a desk and drafting table in the studio, it was a busier place, with scores of apprentices and senior Fellowship members working on projects. Wright wanted a quieter, more ceremonial space where he could greet visitors and clients as well as dictate letters and confer on day-to-day management issues with his then-secretary, Fellowship member and artist Gene Masselink.

Frank Lloyd Wright's Office has been restored to its earlier look, which includes a large table where the architect shared drawings with clients and where his secretary, Gene Masselink, typed letters. LEFT: For several years, the Office became a space used by Taliesin West volunteers and docents, treated here with a coffee break in the 1990s.

Wright placed the office at the edge of the desert camp, making it the first point of contact for anyone visiting the property, and designed it as a separate structure from the studio, allowing the passage between the two nearby buildings to be a time to change gears mentally and physically. The office design served as a microcosm of Wright's approach to desert design, with a low-ceilinged entry that opened up to a larger volume, marked by a roofline angled toward the McDowell Mountains. The building's desert masonry walls link it to the site, and, originally, canvas was stretched between roof beams, giving the office even, filtered light. Wright's signature red concrete floor anchored the space, and a large fireplace kept it warm in the winter. As Taliesin West didn't join the electric grid until about 1950, a generator provided light for a few hours once dusk fell.

While Olgivanna preferred to work on her own projects in the Wright's private quarters, Wright himself had routines in the office, working with Masselink, who tirelessly made everything happen smoothly. The office was Wright's sacred space, and Fellowship members dared not enter unless specifically invited.

Clients and visitors who met here with Wright had to be motivated to come to the then-isolated desert setting, driving a series of tooth-rattling dirt roads, desert washes, and old trails that led from Phoenix to Taliesin West. Even Shea Boulevard, the closest major east-west artery, wasn't fully paved until the 1970s, so the site wasn't easily accessed by tourists or the curious in the early days.

But Wright still proved to be a magnet—and Phoenix was becoming known as a winter resort, so many a dignitary came to call, seeking sun and insight into modern architecture. Elizabeth Gordon visited Wright's office several times. As the editor of *House Beautiful* magazine, she championed his work. Another notable visitor to the office was Anthony Quinn, who had an interest in architecture as a young man before he became a movie star. As the story goes, Quinn traveled by train from Los Angeles to Phoenix and presented his credentials to Wright, hoping to become an apprentice. Wright, however, noticed that Quinn had a speech impediment caused by a too-thick frenum under his tongue. The architect suggested an operation and that Quinn come back when he was able to clearly enunciate his architectural ideas to potential clients. Eventually, Quinn followed the advice and took speech lessons at an acting school, which led him on a different path.

An early rendering of the Office by Jim Thompson shown with stylized saguaro cactus in the background.

After Wright's death in 1959, the office slowly became Taliesin West's administrative center, where Fellowship or family members without an interest in architecture, but who showed a business sense, were gently guided into helping out. The office was no longer a sacred space, but a place where Fellowship members would drop off official requests for purchasing kitchen staples from a wholesale grocer, liquor lists for formal evenings, blueprint orders, sacks of concrete and more. Mail and packages came to the office and were distributed in the mail cubbies in the adjacent Cabaret Theatre. Newspapers were delivered there, and, at the end of the day, when things in the office quieted down, some residents came to read the local *Arizona Republic* or the *Christian Science Monitor* at the coffee table as the late afternoon sun's rays flooded the space through glass doors.

Although the Wrights often lived extravagantly, the couple—and the Fellowship members—were not necessarily known as shrewd businesspeople. Money from projects and apprentice tuition flowed in and flowed out, and, often, creditors threatened to cut the whole crew off. It wasn't until later years that sound accounting practices were introduced in the office, lessening the chance that Arizona Public Service would pull the plug and leave Taliesin West in the dark.

The office was also full of only-in-the-desert quirks. In addition to the occasional reptilian visitor, mice would work their way into the voids of the desert masonry walls and become trapped, dying in what became a Wrightian tomb for the tiny creatures. Fans and open doors helped with the rodential reek, but office workers had to learn to tough things out until the arid desert dried things out. On a more photogenic note, bobcats seemed to be attracted to the office area, often lounging in the shade of nearby trees and cactus. Architect William Wesley Peters became known for his elaborate April Fools' Day pranks, often played out in the office. One involved placing a mouse trap in a glass jar of malted milk balls, awaiting the unwary snacker.

By the 1990s, the office was becoming too crowded; for a time, it was also shared by Bruce Brooks Pfeiffer, author and Taliesin West's historian and archivist, before the archive building was constructed at the edge of the complex. The administrative staff moved into what was once the Wrights' private quarters as well as the original dining room, off the drafting studio. For a few years, the office became a storage facility, crammed with telephone equipment.

Wright used the space to meet with clients, colleagues, and members of the press, including Elizabeth Gordon (above), editor of *House Beautiful*, who championed the architect's work. OPPOSITE: The Wrights outside of the Office in the late 1950s.

However, Taliesin West was quickly becoming a tourist magnet, with visitors from around the world coming to see the buildings and the desert site. What was once an informal operation—a cart with a few books, postcards, and a cashbox—evolved into a major part of life at Taliesin West. Anneliese Dodge, a member of the Fellowship, spearheaded the construction of a bookstore and tour center, where visitors could choose from a roster of guided walks throughout the property. A volunteer program grew from a handful of people who ran the bookstore and gave tours to more than one hundred. The office became the volunteer headquarters, where they could have meetings and check in before heading out on their assignments for the day. It also served as a de facto reception area, where VIP visitors such as fashion journalist Hamish Bowles and author Susan Sontag waited before private tours.

The office has been restored to Wright's early era, albeit with glass in openings where the breezes once blew and more durable acrylic panels for the roof. A few of Wright's treasured Native American and Asian artifacts dot the room. Masselink's vintage Royal typewriter, customized with architectural symbols, and a Rolodex filled with architectural contacts are displayed on a large, low table. Today, the office is the first indoor stop on tours, a place where visitors get an initial sense of Taliesin West's architecture and feel a connection to the site.

The Office, on the far left, is the entry point to Taliesin West's original core and is a few steps away from the Drafting Studio on the right. LEFT: An early view of the Office, from the south.

FOLLOWNG SPREAD: A checkerboard-style awning shades the Office's clerestory window from the afternoon sun, while the plantings of the enclosed courtyard behind the desert masonry walls can be seen.

Cabaret Theatre

For Taliesin West's newly arrived apprentices, the scene must have looked like something out of a fairy tale. Amid candlelight and flowers, men in tuxedos and women in silky evening gowns tucked into dinner and conversed softly. With a backdrop of dramatic rock walls in the partially subterranean setting, a fireplace provided warmth and glow while white twinkling lights, stretched across a rough concrete ceiling, evoked the starry sky of the surrounding desert.

The magical setting, dubbed the Cabaret Theatre, was built between 1949 and 1950 after the Fellowship had outgrown the Kiva Theatre. Designed by Frank Lloyd Wright, it was conceived as a space where the Fellowship could hold their weekly formal evenings and entertain guests—a place for sit-down dinners, small concerts, talks, and film screenings. During those early years, Taliesin West was a fifteen-mile drive down dirt roads to the nearest movie theater, let alone other cultural offerings, inspiring the Fellowship to create its own entertainment venue in the midst of saguaro cactus and brittlebush.

Wright nestled the building into a hillside, sinking it below grade on three sides, hoping apprentices could dig out the site by hand. When shovels hit the Sonoran Desert's

With plush red upholstery, the grotto-like Cabaret Theatre was the site of many Saturday evening formal dinners and other events. RIGHT: Set partially into the ground, the theater was built by members of the Fellowship to Frank Lloyd Wright's design.

FOLLOWING SPREAD: The floor of the Cabaret Theatre slopes, allowing all an unobstructed view of the small stage, where an alcove accommodates the piano. A void under the stage floor acts to enhance the acoustics.

A musical performance in the theater, circa 1950s, marks the end of a formal evening.

ABOVE: Artist Ling Po's place card for a guest at one of the formal evenings. TOP: The large table at the top of the theater was reserved for the Wrights and special guests, and, in later years, for senior members of the Fellowship.

unforgiving, concrete-like caliche, a bulldozer was hired to finish the excavation. In plan, the theater includes a foyer, a small catering kitchen to one side, and an alcove with cubbies where mail was distributed. A long passageway leads to the top of the sloping theater, where rows of seating face the small stage. Along the passageway, a series of wood shutters can be lowered to seal out the bright desert sun. Wright detailed the space with Asian touches, such as the glossy Mandarin-red entry doors bedazzled with elaborate brass hardware, a gong occasionally used to signal dinner, a Buddha head in the foyer, and silk Asian screens once hung from the ceiling. The small stage was designed with an eighteen-inch space beneath its floor, acting like a drum head, moving sound perfectly out into the theater, including music emanating from the grand piano, tucked into a niche.

The architect originally called the theater "Stone Gallery" for the carefully selected large desert rocks that make up the walls, but after the Wrights spent more time in New York working on the Guggenheim Museum, Olgivanna renamed it the Cabaret Theatre, evoking Manhattan's cultural scene. In the early days, the circular head table at the top of the sloping theater had room for the Wrights and a dozen guests. The rest of the apprentices and guests took their seats in forward-facing rows, eating on narrow ledges. Noting how long it took to serve meals to the seated diners, Olgivanna suggested removing every other row and having small drop-leaf tables designed that could accommodate four, seated on upholstered banquettes and Wright-designed chairs. She also became enamored with the white twinkle lights that became popular in the late 1970s, and had them strung on the ceiling after the silk screens had deteriorated.

In the Cabaret Theatre, the dinner component of the Saturday formal evenings worked like a well-oiled machine. Weekly, a young apprentice or senior Fellowship member was assigned to decorate the theater for dinner, creating paper programs outlining the evening's events and place cards for each table, based on a much-negotiated seating chart. Candles and flower arrangements—often culled from the desert and Taliesin West's gardens—were placed on each table. One dinner's notable centerpieces included goldfish circling in the water of the flower vases. The large head table was draped with a handmade tablecloth and set with special Wright-designed Imperial Hotel china, which was stored in a cupboard in the Garden Room. Other tables were set with simple white dishes.

After cocktails in the Garden Room, guests walked past a sculpture of a fire-breathing dragon, through the pergola, along the drafting studio, and into the Cabaret Theatre, scouring the tables for their place cards. Early on, there was a subtle pecking order in the

seating arrangements. The row farthest from the head table was the dining equivalent of Siberia, reserved for new arrivals and children of Fellowship members. The Wrights, and, later, Olgivanna, sat at the head table. Large enough to hold up to fourteen diners, the head table also included some members of the senior Fellowship and perhaps a handful of new apprentices learning the art of table manners and small talk.

The head table was also peppered with esteemed guests important to the Wrights, to Wright's architectural practice, and, in later years, to Taliesin Architects. Over the years, the

A side view of the Cabaret Theatre not long after construction reveals openings that allow light into the entry hallway.

list included a rotating cast of power brokers in business, the arts, and politics, including the Chicago Wrigleys, Encyclopedia Britannica founder and U.S. Senator William Benton, members of the politically prominent Udall family, mayors of Scottsdale and Phoenix, Domino's Pizza founder and Wright enthusiast Tom Monaghan, philanthropist Virginia Ullman, and journalist Mary Hemingway. Despite Olgivanna's strict no-smoking policy for the community, Henry Luce, a frequent guest, famously lit a cigarette at the head table one evening after the dishes were cleared. Olgivanna diplomatically said nothing. In the years after the Wrights passed, the head table was presided over by Dick Carney, who became CEO, and other members of the senior Fellowship. The seating arrangements became more egalitarian, with guests seated among apprentices throughout the theater.

Olgivanna Wright and Fellowship member Dick Carney, who later became CEO of the Frank Lloyd Wright Foundation, pose in front of the Cabaret Theatre's fountain.

Once the guests were seated, four or five apprentices served dinner, which was plated behind a red canvas curtain in the small catering kitchen. Though the menu rotated, the most popular dish was chicken Arlington, basted in orange juice, served with mashed potatoes and green beans. Dessert was often Boston cream pie or chocolate cake. While water was the only beverage served in the early days, Fellowship trips to Europe in the 1960s eased the desert temperance movement; wine was offered at dinner. Among senior Fellowship members and apprentices, it was an open secret that Gallo jug wines or, in later years, budget-friendly box vintages were surreptitiously poured into more impressive bottles served to guests.

Though the dinners in the Cabaret Theatre usually ran like clockwork, there were some crises. During one evening, an apprentice who was serving hurriedly ate his dinner in the kitchen between courses and cleanup. Highly allergic, he discovered part of the meal was cooked in peanut oil. Another server rushed him to the nearest emergency room, and two apprentices were hastily and discreetly pulled into serving roles. During another formal evening, guests had finished cocktails and dinner was already plated when a tremendous rainfall and hailstorm caused flooding between the buildings. Rather than walking outside and wading through calf-deep waters, everyone was led through adjoining buildings to the courtyard outside the Cabaret Theatre, where quick-thinking apprentices had assembled a makeshift bridge from construction forms, and they rolled up their tuxedo trousers to carry gown-clad women into the theater.

Dinner was not the end of the formal evenings. Often, there was a brief concert on the stage, with performances ranging from chamber music to rock songs. (The original grand

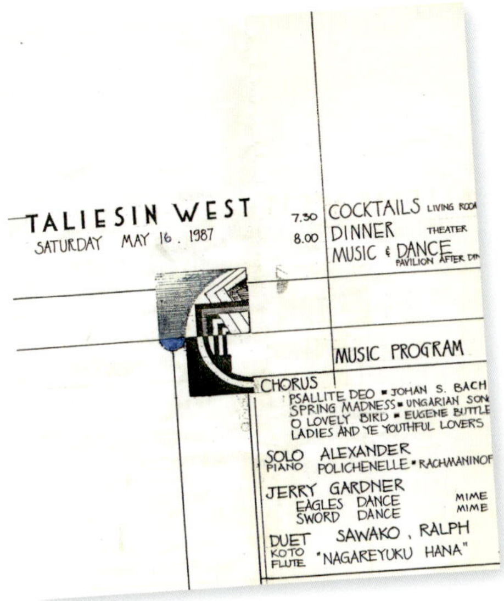

TALIESIN WEST
SATURDAY MAY 16. 1987

7.30 COCKTAILS LIVING ROO
8.00 DINNER THEATER
MUSIC & DANCE PAVILION AFTER DI

MUSIC PROGRAM

CHORUS
PSALLITE DEO • JOHAN S. BACH
SPRING MADNESS • UNGARIAN SON
O LOVELY BIRD • EUGENE BUTTLE
LADIES AND YE YOUTHFUL LOVERS

SOLO ALEXANDER
PIANO POLICHENELLE • RACHMANINOF

JERRY GARDNER
EAGLES DANCE MIME
SWORD DANCE MIME

DUET SAWAKO, RALPH
KOTO
FLUTE "NAGAREYUKU HANA"

CLOCKWISE FROM ABOVE: An apprentice-designed program for a formal evening. An après-dinner concert. Guests and Fellowship members enjoy dinner in the theater. OPPOSITE: While the triangular sconces are original to the theater, the strands of twinkling lights were a later addition and contribute a starry effect to the stone ceiling.

A hallway funnels guests from the entry to the top level the Cabaret Theatre. The ruddy-hued shutters along the bottom of the rock wall can be flipped up to block daylig in the theater.

piano, tucked into an alcove, proved to be the perfect nesting spot for desert pack rats, who filled it with spiky cholla sections during summers when the Fellowship migrated to Taliesin in Wisconsin. The piano was replaced, and covered securely for the summer season.)

After the concerts, movies were shown, run with professional equipment from the projection booth behind the head table. Wright was keen on American movies (particularly since his granddaughter, actress Anne Baxter, was a popular film star), favoring Westerns and classics, provided to him weekly by his Hollywood connections, while Olgivanna leaned toward Russian and European cinematic offerings. In later years, Fellowship members sat in the darkened theater to enjoy the latest popular films, including Oscar-winning titles and indie favorites.

After the Saturday night formals, the Cabaret Theatre did not sit empty all week. There were other performances and recitals in the space, including those by some high-profile entertainers. English actor Charles Laughton, enamored with Wright's work, spent a week at Taliesin West, and recited Bible verses, Shakespeare, and Dickens in the small theater to an enraptured Fellowship. The Fellowship's tradition of putting together humorous skits—often gently skewering one other—frequently took place in the theater.

When Taliesin West opened for public tours in the 1970s, architect Charles Schiffner crafted a wooden cart to hold books, postcards, and a cashbox for tour payments that was stored in the mailbox alcove and wheeled outside to greet visitors.

Today, a full-scale bookstore and tour-ticket kiosk has replaced the cart. The Cabaret Theatre is still in use, for informal events such as lectures, small concerts, and films. It's also the last stop on tours, offering visitors a cool, dark place to contemplate life at Taliesin West.

A view of the Cabaret Theatre soon after construction reveals its sunken setting.
LEFT: Congresswoman, ambassador, and playwright Clare Boothe Luce, Olgivanna Wright, and *Time* magazine founder Henry Luce at a formal evening. The Luces, who had a winter home in Phoenix, were frequent guests at Taliesin West.

Pavilion

On Thursday, September 26, 1963, Taliesin West was coming back to life as groups of Fellowship members returned after spending the summer at Taliesin in Spring Green, Wisconsin. Though the desert's summer monsoons had waned, it was breezy and the temperature had climbed to a toasty 105 degrees when an enormous ball of smoke and flames arose from the Pavilion building. Senior Fellowship member and architect Charles Montooth was the first to see the conflagration and attempted to put out the flames with a fire extinguisher. He was soon joined by other Fellowship members who formed a bucket brigade to fight the spreading catastrophe before it was extinguished by the Rural Fire Protection Company, which sent six trucks up the hill to quell the blaze.

By night, all that was left standing were the Pavilion's desert masonry walls, while its canvas roof and wood beams were burnt to ash. In the local paper, the *Arizona Republic*, Olgivanna speculated that the cause of the fire was possibly spontaneous combustion, in a pile of sheet music stored in the orchestra pit, or in a tangle of velour draperies stacked near the stage. Privately, though, she and the Fellowship members guessed a wayward cigarette caused the disaster.

Lacquered red doors lead into the Pavilion, Taliesin West's largest theater. ABOVE: The first version of the Pavilion, designed by Frank Lloyd Wright and built in 1957, burned in 1963 and was rebuilt eighteen months later.

With can-do spirit, the Fellowship cleared the site and, under direction from chief architect William Wesley Peters, they rebuilt this Taliesin West theater with a steel beam system and a fiber glass roof. It opened some eighteen months later in April 1965 for another iteration of Taliesin West's Festival of Music and Dance.

The original Pavilion was completed in 1957, the last building at Taliesin West designed and overseen by Frank Lloyd Wright. With the growth of the Fellowship and more public involvement, Wright decided that his desert community needed a proper performance space. In essence, though, it was designed to showcase the musical and choreographic talents of Wright's daughter with Olgivanna, Iovanna. Like her mother, Iovanna had become interested in the teachings of philosopher-mystic George Gurdjieff and was sent to Paris to study at his center in the late 1940s. In France, she learned Gurdjieff's movements, or dances, said to enhance a higher state of consciousness.

Back home in the desert and inspired by Gurdjieff, Iovanna began staging elaborate dance and music productions, complete with costumes and stage sets, under Olgivanna's watchful eye. Much of the Fellowship was involved, with many a late-night rehearsal. The performances were held outdoors on a concrete slab until the Pavilion was built.

Both the original and rebuilt Pavilion were similar in design, with some one-hundred-plus red-upholstered seats in rows that rise steeply to an upper-level lounge area and fireplace.

ABOVE: With the Fellowship's construction expertise, the Pavilion rose again shortly after the fire. RIGHT: The Pavilion provides a spacious setting for everything from lectures to dance performances. The floor in the foreground opens to reveal an orchestra pit, while the colorful arch to the left is a reproduction of a design by Wright for Midway Gardens in Chicago.

The orchestra pit was designed to be covered if more stage area was needed, and the depth of the stage was controlled by a series of curtains, suspended on pivoting poles. To one side of the stage, what looks like a puppet theater is a decorative, miniaturized arched mural based on Wright's design for Midway Gardens in Chicago. At the back of the theater on a wall, a quote from the Chinese philosopher Lao Tzu reads "The reality of the building does not consist in roof and walls, but in the space within to be lived in." (Wright, occasionally taking liberties with history and names, spelled the philosopher's name "Laotse" on the wall.)

From the 1950s into the '70s, Taliesin West's annual spring Festival of Music and Dance took place on the Pavilion stage and proved to be popular with the public, who purchased tickets for the showcase. With dances choreographed by Iovanna and performed by her and members of the Fellowship, as well as music written by Olgivanna, the festival was a visual feast, with costumes, intricate hand-built sets, and theatrical lighting.

Early performances in the Pavilion included hand-crafted sets and costumes, sketched out here. RIGHT: Olgivanna Wright enjoys a Twelfth Night gala with Henry Luce, a frequent guest, in the Pavilion.

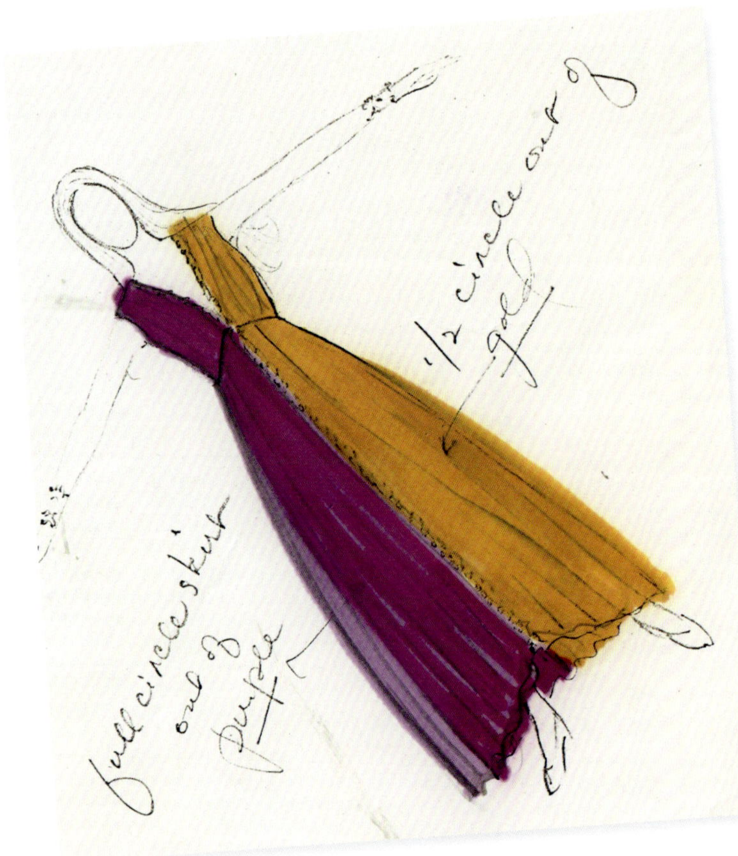

Originally designed to showcase the theatrical talents of the Wrights' daughter, Iovanna, the Pavilion was the site of the annual Festival of Music and Dance.

Nearly everyone in the Fellowship, from young apprentices to senior architects, participated in the Festival of Music and Dance, either behind the scenes or as performers.

With a translucent ceiling, the Pavilion could be used day or night. The depth of the stage is controlled by a series of draperies, hung from pivoting poles. TOP: Looking northeast, the Pavilion's form echoes that of nearby mountains. BELOW: A cross-section of the theater reveals its roof design.

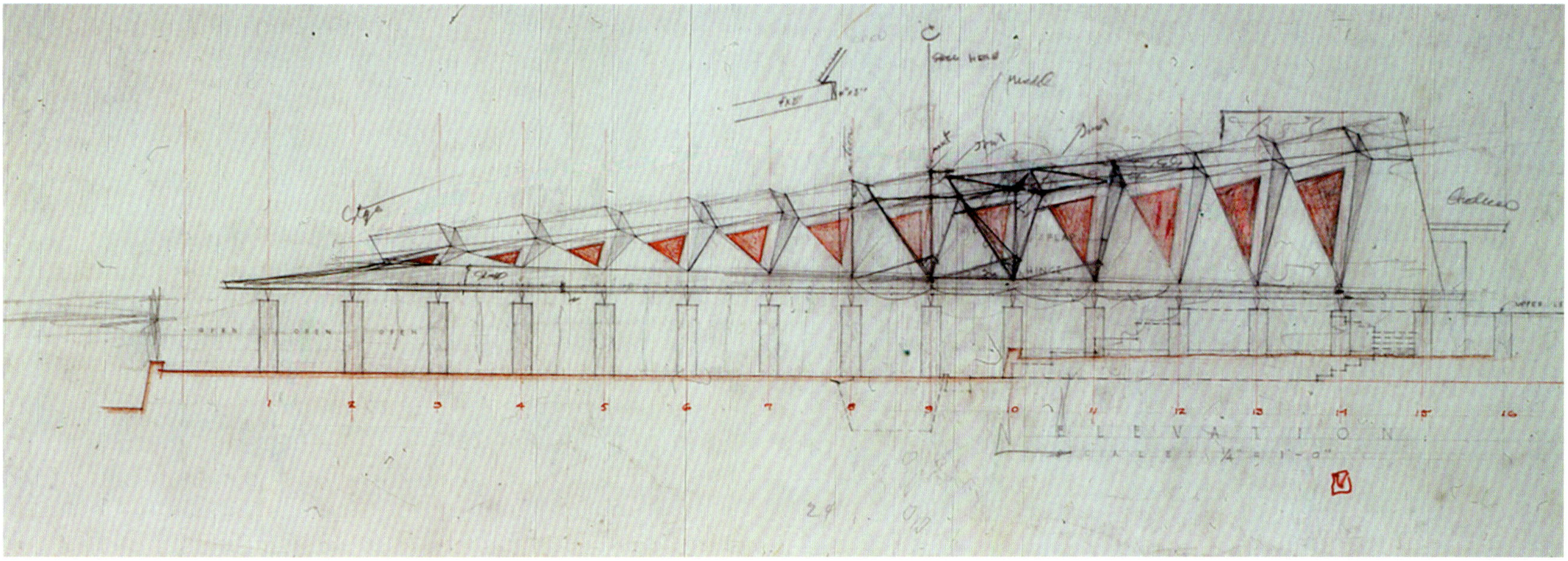

Taliesin's orchestra takes to the Pavilion stage during a Twelfth Night celebration.

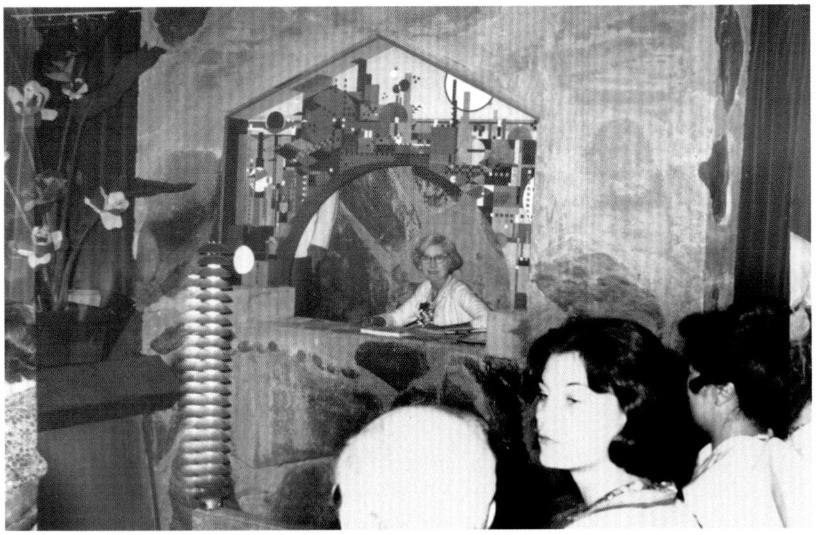

Tucked into the Pavilion's arch, Clare Booth Luce watches the reading of her new play in the early 1960s.

However, the Pavilion was in use for more than just one event a year. With an emphasis on the arts—particularly music—the community encouraged new apprentices to join the Fellowship's chorus, recorder group, string ensemble, and, in later years, even a rock band, all of which performed regularly during formal evenings. More Gurdjieff-inspired dance programs were later led by artist Heloise Christa after Iovanna's mental health challenges diminished her artistry. Even new apprentices who lacked musical talent were encouraged to quietly sing in the back row of the chorus or don a funny wig to participate in humorous skits presented on the Pavilion stage, with the hope of exposing them to new experiences. Even in the 1960s, the Pavilion's stage was open to outside talent invited to perform by the Fellowship, including Clare Boothe Luce, who oversaw a reading of her new play.

The Pavilion also served as the backdrop for Taliesin West's annual Twelfth Night holiday event in January, when the space was filled with candlelit tables, twinkling lights, icicle decor, and more for dinner and musical interludes performed by the Fellowship. If the weather on Easter Sunday proved to be too hot or too cold, the breakfast was moved into the Pavilion, made bright with dyed eggs and balloons. Starting in the 1980s, apprentices began presenting their Box Projects, an architectural or artistic study done twice a year, for critiques and approval in the Pavilion.

Others, besides the Fellowship, made themselves at home in the Pavilion, not only for performances. During one lecture, an eagle-eyed apprentice saw something moving on the stage behind a speaker at the lectern, quietly went backstage and moved the curtains to conceal the rattlesnake, which was quickly relocated outdoors. During other performances, astute audience members could make out the outlines of a raccoon-like ringtail cat padding across the translucent roof.

More recently, the Pavilion has been used for lectures, classes, and workshops. Southwest Shakespeare Company has presented works by the Bard in the auditorium, and the stage has seen performances by Arizona Opera and other theatrical groups. Music, poetry, and film screenings also take place in the Pavilion; many of the events are open to the public.

The fire in 1963, it seems, was just a small setback.

Outdoor Spaces

On Easter Sunday morning, dozens of large round tables dot the gravel walkway of the Prow, the triangular terrace and garden space that rises above the desert floor. Children, dressed in spring finery, search the grass and bushes for hidden Easter eggs, being careful not to fall into the shallow, triangle-shaped pool in the center. Adults gather around the tables, bedecked with dozens of colored eggs, jellybeans, Jordan almonds and vases filled with flowers, along with chubby towers of sweet baba bread and bowls of creamy paska cheese—nods to Olgivanna Wright's Slavic roots.

After breakfast, members of the Fellowship gather up the multicolored, helium-filled balloons that decorate the garden, tie them together and attach a self-addressed, stamped post-card to the strand. Before FAA or environmental concerns, the enormous balloon bouquet would be released, in hopes that the finder would mail back the postcard with details as to where the deflated balloons landed. Over the years, returned cards bore postmarks in distant parts of Arizona, New Mexico, and even Arkansas.

A recent aerial view of Taliesin West reveals its numerous outdoor settings, including the V-shaped Prow in the foreground and, to the right, shallow steps leading up to the red concrete Sunset Terrace. ABOVE: Olgivanna Wright, center, greets guests on the Sunset Terrace during an Easter breakfast, Taliesin's largest social event of the year.

Easter, a gathering of the Fellowship, family, and friends, was by far Taliesin West's largest event, held annually for decades for up to two hundred people and almost always taking place on the Prow, weather permitting. As much thought as Frank Lloyd Wright put into the buildings of the desert site, he also spent a great deal of time with the outdoor spaces around the buildings, such as the Prow, knowing that life in a desert climate blurred the line between indoors and out.

Though most of the Taliesin West site was natural Sonoran Desert, Wright began adding cultivated pockets of hardscape and plantings early on. One of the first areas to be designed was the Prow, from which he could gaze out on the desert below and city lights in the distance, noting that it was like "standing on the rim of the world." While the Prow's small lawn and shallow reflecting pool provided a cooling foreground for the adjacent studio, kitchen, and dining room, the pool's existence was for more than aesthetics and wading. It provided a ready water source to fight fires in the early days when city services were far away.

The Sunset Terrace, a few steps up from the Prow and directly adjacent to the Garden Room and the Wrights' private quarters, provided even better views of desert and city below. A shaded, cooling Breezeway was also built under Wright's supervision, connecting the dining area with the Wrights' private quarters. The master architect also designed the redwood

An axial perspective Frank Lloyd Wright drawing shows details for the landscaping of the Prow and other outdoor spaces.

FOLLOWING SPREAD: Nestled into the Prow's lawn, the triangular-shaped pool serves as a cooling element in the landscape. In the early days, when Taliesin West was far from city services, it served as a water source to fight fires.

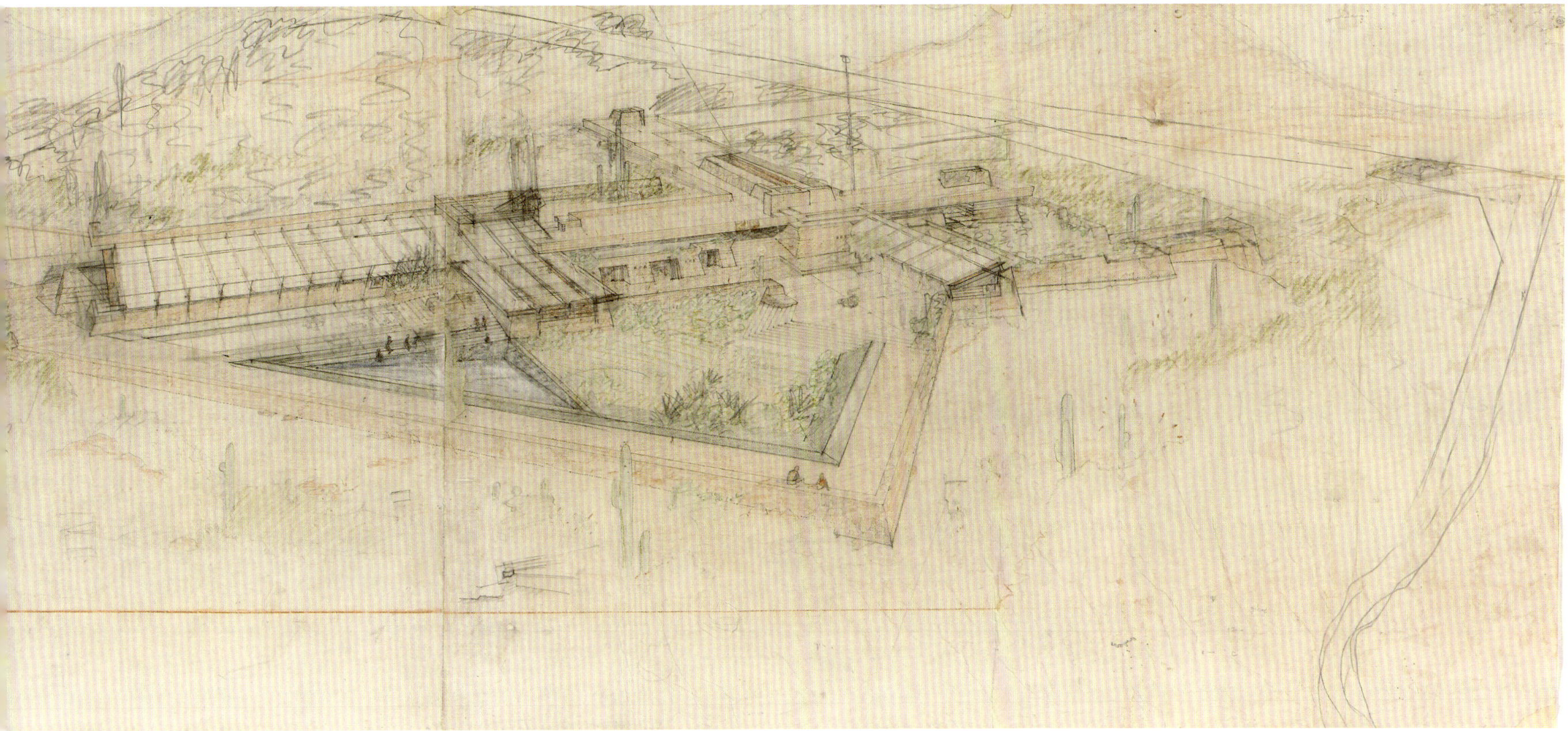

Pergola, a sheltered passageway along the north side of the Drafting Studio, which provides an ever-changing pattern of light and shadow. Far from being content with hardscape structures alone, Wright incorporated art—antique and ancient—into the garden settings, including his collection of antique Chinese ceramic friezes and boulders bearing petroglyphs, remnants from the lives of indigenous people who once passed through the site.

The plant palette for the outdoor spaces evolved organically. At first, the Fellowship used whatever was at hand to save money, digging up cactus and desert shrubs to fill planter beds and heal construction scars, unwittingly being at the cutting edge of the trend to revegetate the land with native species. After World War II, Wright wanted to soften garden spots closer to the buildings and drove down to Phoenix with a handful of apprentices to buy out nurseries of then-popular plant materials to experiment with in desert soils.

There were hits and misses. Palm trees thought to grow low and stubby soon towered over the Taliesin West buildings—out of scale—and were removed. After several women complained that their formal gowns kept getting snagged on the cholla that lined the Pergola as they walked to and from the Saturday evening formal dinners, apprentices were tasked with digging up the spiky cactus and replacing them with dozens of magenta-hued bougainvillea.

CLOCKWISE FROM TOP LEFT: Frank Lloyd Wright enjoys dappled sunlight outdoors. The Wrights partake in the Easter breakfast in the late 1950s on the Sunset Terrace. Children hunt for Easter eggs on the Prow in the 1960s. 1940s-era tea on the Sunset Terrace.

Flowers, mostly picked from the desert and Taliesin West's cultivated gardens, fill a fountain during an Easter breakfast.

Frank Lloyd Wright incorporated antique Chinese friezes and boulders bearing petroglyphs found on site into garden walls.

Flanked by towering Easter babas, the Wrights enjoy the annual springtime social event at Taliesin West.

Pyracantha shrubs were planted in front of the Drafting Studio's windows after a child accidentally walked through the frameless glass. Oleander, cypress, junipers, myrtle, pomegranates, arborvitae, jacaranda, hibiscus, and other non-natives soon transitioned from nursery containers to flourishing flora in nooks and crannies around the site. When Wright grew tired of driving down to his son David Wright's home in a citrus grove in Phoenix to gather fruit, he plotted a citrus grove to the north of the Drafting Studio, which was planted after his death with grapefruit, juice oranges, tangerines, limes, lemons, and more. Nearby, several members of the Fellowship planted vegetable gardens.

By the late 1980s, with a movement toward the use of desert-friendly species, arid-region plants such as yellow yucca, chuparosa, Mexican honeysuckle, octopus agave, and various sages began cropping up around new construction and restoration projects, replacing plants that required more water.

Maintenance of the growing panoply of plant material largely fell to young apprentices, supervised by senior members of the Fellowship, including Cornelia Brierly, Frances and Stephen Nemtin, and Tony Putnam, who showed an affinity for landscape design. There was grass to be mowed, hedges to be trimmed, flora to fertilize, citrus to harvest, and flowers to pick for dinner tables. Some apprentices looked forward to being outdoors as opposed to a kitchen-duty assignment. Others took it as benign torture, particularly when caught in a crossfire of opinions as to how much a tree, hedge, or shrub should be trimmed. Architect William Wesley Peters was particularly finicky about how white holiday lights should be installed in the Pergola's bougainvillea, directing apprentices to tuck the strands deep into the vines' thorny branches, resulting in a run on Band-Aids.

The entry courtyard between the Drafting Studio and the Cabaret Theatre was often set for special events, such as wedding receptions.

FOLLOWING TWO SPREADS:

The Prow's gravel walkway, flanked by yellow-blooming brittlebush, agaves, and bougainvillea, offers views of Scottsdale in the distance.

More Chinese ceramics and Frank Lloyd Wright's signature red ceramic square mark the entrance to the Garden Room off the Sunset Terrace.

The citrus grove and vegetable garden were often maintained by techniques not seen as acceptable by today's standards. Fellowship members, armed with pellet guns and rifles, were not shy about picking off interlopers. Still, birds, javelina, rabbits, and deer usually won out. The vegetable gardens were given up, and it became an accepted fact that a percentage of the citrus had to be shared with desert creatures.

In the summer, a skeleton crew of Fellowship members kept the gardens alive, sometimes aided by Olgivanna's brother, known as Uncle Vlado, and his wife, Sophie, who would visit for long periods, staying in the guest quarters above the dining room. Vlado, too, was known to wield a rifle, though not at furry or feathered friends, but rather at two-legged types who tried to sneak onto Taliesin West property, thinking it was abandoned in the heat of summer. Vlado was said to have fired warning shots more than once.

Water has always been a luxury in the desert, and Wright quickly learned the cooling effect of pools and fountains, which he incorporated into Taliesin West's design. In addition to the triangular fountain on the Prow, a shallow geometric pool delineates a walkway past the Kiva to the Fellowship apartments of the Apprentice Court. Another fountain splashes by what is now the Frank Lloyd Wright Store. The circular fountain between the Office and Cabaret Theatre was a hastily improvised water feature devised by Wright to impress a visitor. After Wright's passing and as the Fellowship's season in Arizona expanded, an in-ground swimming pool was added for all to enjoy. Cornelia Brierly built a small private swimming

pool in the back of her apartment, as did archivist Bruce Brooks Pfeiffer when he built his own home on Taliesin West's grounds. After Wright's death, Olgivanna followed Phoenix landscape trends and had the triangular pool and fountains re-plastered from their original concrete to blue, giving the water a resort-like turquoise hue. They have since been restored to the concrete plaster.

Taliesin West residents made good use of the precious waters, often gathering for pool parties at the Fellowship pool and enjoying the cooling sights and sounds of the fountains. Animals, too, have come to enjoy the waters. Particularly during the heat of the summer, bobcats, deer, and even a stealthy mountain lion or two have been known to quench their thirst at the fountains.

In between planting, trimming, and splashing, the Fellowship and guests made use of the outdoor spaces within the site. In addition to Easter, the Prow was the site of many dinners, weddings, and receptions. The dramatic steps leading from the studio down to the Prow have been the site of many a Fellowship group photo. The Sunset Terrace was a traditional gathering place for the Fellowship's afternoon tea, where members enjoyed rocking gently on patio gliders and chatting with the Wrights. In later years, the terrace was also a gathering spot for cocktails and buffets. The adjacent breezeway, warmed by a fireplace, doubled as a place for tea or smaller group events if the weather was inclement. It was there that actress Loretta Young and her entourage encountered a large tarantula, moving at a leisurely gait across the concrete floor. It's said that a woman in her group wanted to capture the arachnid and take it home, as some kind of Sonoran souvenir. Though designed as a passageway, the Pergola was also put to use as a dining space for special events, with long tables set end to end down its length.

The Taliesin West gardens were used for some out-of-the-ordinary artistic happenings, including a performance of taiko drummers on the Prow one Easter and the use of the Pergola by an avant-garde musical ensemble, which incorporated the structure's beams into a concert. The 1990s Ken Burns documentary on Frank Lloyd Wright had a premiere at Taliesin West, screened outdoors on a gravel courtyard next to the citrus orchard. More recently, Dale Chihuly's art glass sculptures were embedded into the landscape during a special exhibit.

An early view of Taliesin West shows the use of native desert plants for the landscape, including cholla, yucca, and the tall saguaro cactus. In later years, traditional nursery stock was added to soften the gardens closer to the buildings.

Along the Drafting Studio, the Pergola shows off an intricate shadow pattern and neatly trimmed bougainvillea. The walkway has been used for outdoor dinners and even performances. RIGHT: The Prow proved to be the perfect outdoor stage for a chorus performance.

FOLLOWING SPREAD: As viewed from the second-story guest quarters, the Sunset Terrace is a popular spot for outdoor social events with city lights as the backdrop.

Today, outdoor spaces at Taliesin West are still very much in use. In addition to tours, there are regularly scheduled yoga, meditation, and tai chi classes on property, as well as public happy hours, "Sunsets and Sips." Private events, including dinners, cocktail receptions, and wedding ceremonies, are scheduled throughout the gardens. And, the Prow, it turns out, has become a popular backdrop for many a heartfelt event—marriage proposals.

NO VISITORS BEYOND
THIS POINT

A view above blooming aloes shows the kitchen's bell tower and antique Chinese ceramics embedded into a staircase wall. The Dining Room is to the left. ABOVE: With the water tower as a backdrop, the gravel courtyard is the setting for many outdoor dinners.

Rendering of Taliesin West site ca. 1962, by Allen Lape "Davy" Davison, Vern Swaback, and Dan Novak, members of the Taliesin Fellowship.

Shelters

Along the edge of a dry wash north of the buildings of Taliesin West, a group of apprentices gathered at night in a tent, illuminated by a kerosene lantern. Outside, a mesquite wood campfire provided warmth and a place to cook hotdogs. As the moon rose over the McDowell Mountains, a pack of coyotes yipped in the distance. The voices of the apprentices drifted across the desert, accompanied by the clink of beer bottles and the sound of laughter.

From its earliest days, Taliesin West was first and foremost a camp. Early Fellowship members slept on bedrolls on the desert floor and, later, in tents, as the buildings were constructed. Even after rooms, apartments, and cottage-like homes were built, first-year apprentices were instructed to find a site, pitch a tent, and learn about nature *in situ*. In later years, building a more elaborate shelter out in the desert was considered a hands-on learning experience to understand architecture, engineering, and construction.

When Frank Lloyd Wright and the Fellowship arrived to Taliesin West's desert site in 1937, the camping situation was a matter of trial and error. Bedrolls on the ground like in those depicted in popular Hollywood Westerns seemed great, but the reality of scorpions, rattlesnakes, tarantulas, and other desert denizens quickly led to other solutions, such as wooden sleeping boxes with protective sides, utilized by Wright and Olgivanna—unless they decamped to an inn in distant Phoenix. Wright, however, found a long-term solution when he noticed that the Basque shepherds who used nearby desert trails to run flocks between pastures made use of tetrahedron-shaped canvas tents for sleeping. Wright obtained several tents and doled them out to Fellowship members, thus planting the seeds of Taliesin West's shelter tradition.

Flanked by desert trees, a newer shelter emerges from a previous desert masonry base and makes use of rope webbing. BELOW: An aerial view of Taliesin West, likely late 1950s or early 1960s, shows the desert north of the buildings dotted with the traditional white tents.

While at first tent sites encircled the site's core, Wright thought the white canvas forms detracted from views of the

Tent sites evolved into more permanent shelters, making use of materials such as concrete blocks.

mountains and the newly constructed buildings. He relocated the tents to the northern third of the property, following the curves of a wash that carries rainwater runoff from the McDowells. Hung upon a metal frame, the original tents were ten feet by ten feet, just large enough for a single bed, a small table, and a chair. The tent sites became more permanent as concrete or stone platforms were added, while others sported wooden bases. By the 1940s, apartments and rooms were built, giving seasoned apprentices and senior members of the Fellowship first dibs on traditional living accommodations. Many chose to stay out in the desert—some for decades. In the early years, both male and female apprentices slept in the tents. When rooms became available, women were offered those spaces in what was considered an act of chivalry. Many declined and went for the full desert experience.

The original tents had (almost) all the comforts of home. By the 1980s, many of the shelters became even more experimental, utilizing soaring roof planes and intricate triangular panels.

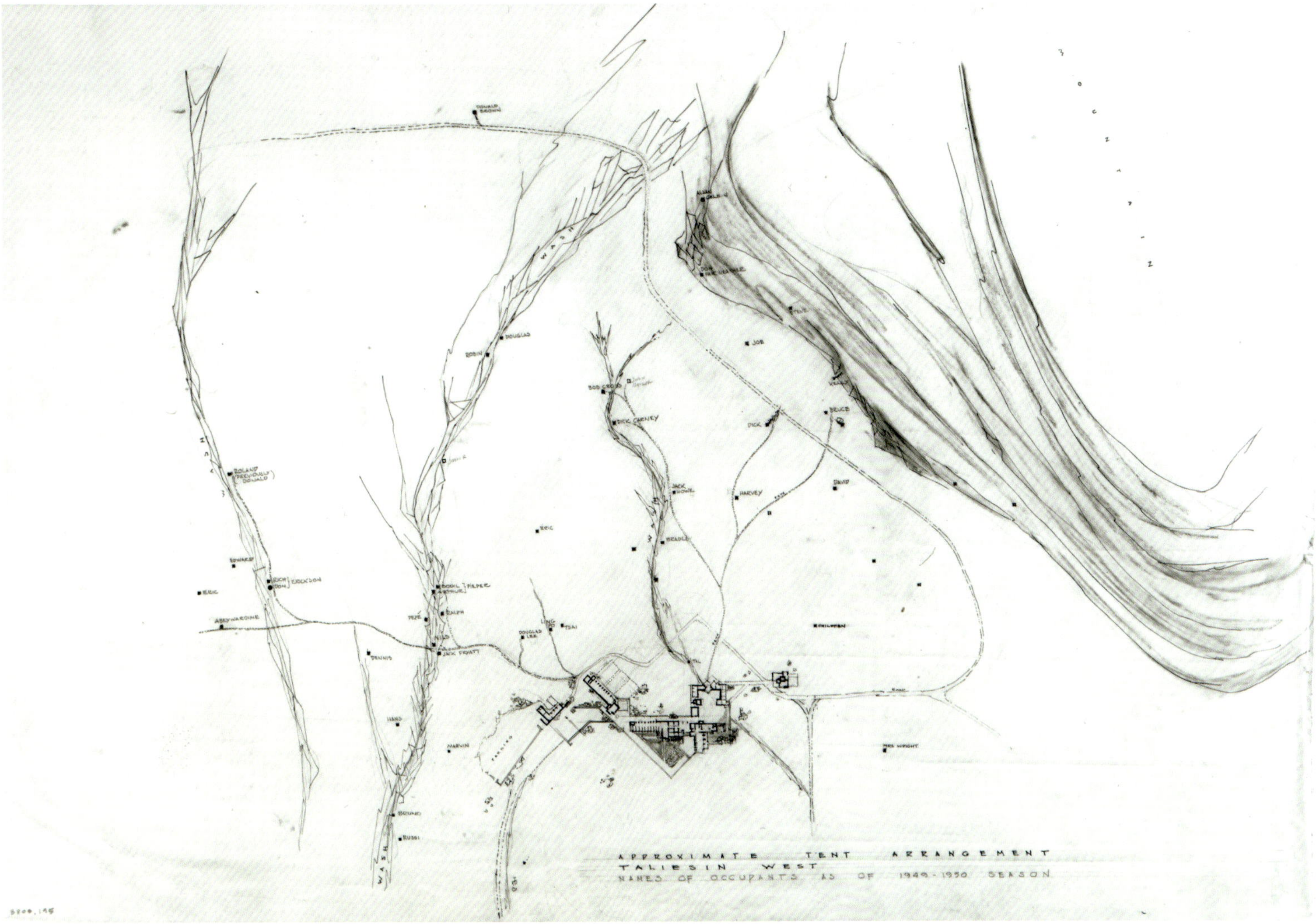

A map from Taliesin West's 1949–1950 season plots out tent locations and their occupants. FAR LEFT: An angled roofline and a cantilevered deck mark one shelter. LEFT: Fellowship members Minerva and Charles Montooth and their children pose in their larger tent, circa 1960s.

A two-level shelter rises from its serene desert setting.

Experimentation was always encouraged in shelter construction, such as the use of rammed earth to build this minimalist structure.

A traditional Taliesin West tent glows lantern-like against the night sky.

Senior members of the Fellowship tackled larger shelters or even small homes in the desert. Architect Stephen Nemtin and landscape designer Frances Nemtin's shelter included core materials such as articulated block, flagstone, and an arched roof structure.

By the 1960s, some of the tent sites became more permanent shelters, as Fellowship members carved out time to build something of their own, scrounging materials in the scrap yard behind Taliesin West's shop, fishing up donations or funding the construction themselves. Desert masonry, metal, canvas, glass, wood, and other materials were used, and the shelters became more elaborate, sporting sleeping and living areas, fireplaces, and cantilevered terraces. It was a hands-on learning experience to understand what worked in the arid environment.

In the early 1960s, Kamal Amin, an apprentice who stayed on to become an architect with Taliesin Architects, built one of the first elaborate shelters for a female apprentice with whom he was enamored. Dubbed Lotus Shelter, the curved block structure features a petal-like roof and opens toward the morning sun. Other impressive shelters followed, each reflecting the personality of the builder. After the apprenticeship program became an accredited school, shelter-building became part of the curriculum, with modern designs and new materials tested, including rammed earth, straw bale, and tensile fabrics. It was a chance for young architects in training to come up with a concept, have it reviewed and approved by senior architects, and experience constructing the idea. Some of the newer shelters were published in design magazines, helping to launch budding architecture careers. One from the early 2000s, Hanging Tent, with a form like the original shepherd's tent that appears to be suspended over the desert floor, received a lot of press.

By the 1990s, there were roughly one hundred tent and shelter sites scattered throughout the property. A moratorium was declared on new sites, and apprentices took over existing shelters, restoring or rebuilding them after the original occupants had moved on. Still, others continued to ask for the traditional tents, custom-made for Taliesin West by a local tent and awning company as replacements for ones that had worn out.

Day-to-day life in the shelters was equal parts magic and challenges. There was the romance of the desert at night, the moon, and the brilliant stars, dimmed a bit by Scottsdale's suburban spread that began in the 1970s. There was the distinctly refreshing smell of the creosote bush after a rain, the peace and quiet after a long day of work duties and studio time, the glimpses of deer and even feral burros, abandoned by miners and ranchers years ago. There were the parties, many of them, hosted by apprentices in their tents or shelters, which the senior members of the Fellowship learned not to crash unless specifically invited.

But it was the desert. Apprentices learned not to touch the canvas of tents during a rainstorm lest a leak occur. They also learned to memorize the location of their sleeping quarters—the tents and shelters stretched nearly a half mile north of the main buildings and there were no trail markers. More than one apprentice spent time in the dark briefly lost. Besides hissing snakes under beds, desert toads, spiders, and scorpions, there were other creatures. One apprentice, sleeping on an open-air platform before his shelter was completed, awoke to a herd of javelinas thundering around his platform. Another, opening up the flap to his tent at night, saw a pair of yellow eyes blinking in the flashlight beam from atop his sleeping bag. The panicked bobcat lunged past the startled apprentice to get out.

OPPOSITE: Fabric artist and tent designer Bill Moss found inspiration and kindred spirits after a season spent at Taliesin West in the early 1990s, giving birth to these artistic tensile fabric structures. RIGHT: "Hanging Tent," inspired by the original tents, was one of the most photographed shelters in the 2000s. BELOW: A circular form and a platform is all that's needed to sleep.

FOLLOWING SPREAD: Cholla cactus and yellow-blooming paloverde trees encroach on an unused shelter foundation.

Social gatherings of apprentices in tents and shelters were common over the decades.

Packrats were also the bane of unwary desert dwellers who quickly learned how to live with the clever rodents. When an apprentice couldn't find his watch and wallet left in his shelter, he began searching the nearby grounds and found his gnawed wallet and ID card used as part of the facade of a packrat midden, or nest, built of spiky cholla segments. He dismantled the nest with a shovel as an act of revenge. Others resorted to sprinkling mothballs around their quarters as a way to discourage unwanted roommates. After an encounter, apprentices knew to keep personal objects safe in the nearby locker rooms where they also showered.

Shelters and tents could also be flammable. One canvas tent went up in flames from a close encounter with a lantern; one straw bale shelter burned when the wiring to solar panels shorted, likely chewed by packrats. Luckily, there were no serious injuries.

Occasionally, after a few too many encounters with nature or heavy rains, some apprentices took to sleeping in the student lounge, which sometimes looked like a youth hostel. Some apprentices made a beeline for rooms and apartments when they became available. Still others remained in tents and shelters, preferring the adventure.

Today, some of the older tent sites and shelters now sprout brittlebush shrubs and paloverde trees, having been swallowed up by the desert. Others have withstood the test of time.

Many of the shelters became house-like, with patios, windows, and doors.

As the apprentice program and school are no longer part of Taliesin West, plans are underway for the Taliesin Institute, a new educational program that offers documentation and restoration opportunities at the shelters for students. Visitors can also take part in seasonal tours of some of the shelter and tent sites.

A boulder with petroglyphs serves as a reminder of the land's ancient history and marks the entry to the Pergola.

W E S T

Selected Bibliography

Arizona Republic, September 26, 1963, weather report.

Arizona Republic, September 27, 1963, "$150,000 Damage Estimated, Fire Sears Taliesin West," 1–2.

Arizona Republic, February 19, 1965, "Rebuilding Pavilion," 4.

Arizona Republic, April 29, 1965, "New Dance-Drama by Iovanna Wright to Open Rebuilt Taliesin Pavilion," 67.

Arizona State University Library archives, Continuing the legacy: The Taliesin Associated Architects collection. https://lib.asu.edu/news/continuing-legacy-taliesin-associated-architects-collection.

Besinger, Curtis. *Working with Mr. Wright: What It Was Like*. Cambridge, England: Cambridge University Press, 1995.

Brierly, Cornelia. *Tales of Taliesin*. Tempe: Arizona State University Herberger Center for Design Excellence in Collaboration with the Frank Lloyd Wright Foundation, 1999.

Frances Nemtin memoirs, housed at the Taliesin West William Wesley Peters Library.

Nemtin, Frances. *The Taliesin Fellowship Festival of Music and Dance*. Madison, WI: The Printing Partners, 2009.

Taliesin West cookbooks, housed at the Taliesin West William Wesley Peters Library.

Taliesin West Plant List, compiled by Jake Maher, landscape consultant, housed at the Taliesin West William Wesley Peters Library.

Taliesin West Preservation Master Plan, Abridged Version. https://franklloydwright.org/wp-content/uploads/2017/01/Taliesin-West-Preservation-Master-Plan_Abridged_copyright-2015-Frank-Lloyd-Wright-Foundation.pdf.

Trulsson, Nora Burba. *Architectural Record*, April 27, 2022, "Former Taliesin School of Architecture Grows New Roots at Paolo Solieri's Arcosanti." https://www.architecturalrecord.com/articles/15634-former-taliesin-school-of-architecture-grows-new-roots-at-paolo-soleris-arcosanti.

Whirling Arrow weekly newsletters, housed at the Taliesin West William Wesley Peters Library.

The entrance to Taliesin West is marked by an abstraction of Frank Lloyd Wright's "whirling arrow" symbol, a petroglyph-inspired design that Wright thought looked like two hands clasped together in friendship.

Acknowledgments

Working on this project was an emotional voyage for me—I met my husband, Jorgen Ove Trulsson, just outside the Pavilion at Taliesin West in 1985, and it was at Frank Lloyd Wright's "desert camp" that we married and started our family. So many people we met there became lifelong friends and encouraged me with this book, sharing memories, photographs, contact information, and more, with countless emails, interviews, and Zoom calls.

First and foremost, I am indebted to Stuart Graff, president and CEO of the Frank Lloyd Wright Foundation, and Douglas Curran, my editor at Rizzoli, for finding me and guiding me through the process. Thank you to Andrew Pielage for sharing his magnificent photographs of Taliesin West as it appears today. Also, a thanks to David Skolkin for his beautiful graphic design.

Going above and beyond in helping me with the book were Indira Berndtson, Effi Casey, Elizabeth Dawsari, Floyd Hamblen, Minerva Montooth, Oskar Munoz, Fred Prozzillo, Arnold Roy, and Margo Stipe of the Frank Lloyd Wright Foundation, whose expertise with history, research, and photography—as well as decades spent living and working at Taliesin West—kept the project on the straight and narrow.

For sharing memories of life at Taliesin West, along with snapshots, I'd like to thank Anna Coor, Alexander Dodge, Kempton Fuller, Aris Georges, Ron Haynes, Stuart Henderson, Bing Hu, Margo Montooth, Jerry Morosco, Suzi Pace, Natascha Payton, Tom Payton, Erik Peterson, Michael Rust, John Sather, Adrienne Schiffner, Pamela Penn Sprenger, Rod Tuenge, and Jochen Walter.

Finally, a big thank-you to family and friends who were patient with me as I disappeared into this book project.

Contributors

Nora Burba Trulsson is an Arizona-based architecture, design, and travel writer, and a former member of the Taliesin Fellowship. Her work has appeared in *Architectural Record*, *Phoenix Home & Garden*, *California Homes*, *Sunset*, *Arizona Highways*, the *Chicago Tribune* and numerous other publications. She has co-authored several books, including *Desert Southwest*, *Desert Southwest Gardens*, and *Living Homes: Sustainable Architecture and Design*.

Andrew Pielage is an internationally published architectural and travel photographer based in Phoenix, Arizona, on a mission to photograph all remaining Frank Lloyd Wright designs. His work for Rizzoli includes *50 Lessons to Learn from Frank Lloyd Wright*.

Growing up in Chicago, **Stuart Graff** began studying Frank Lloyd Wright's work more than fifty years ago, sustaining a lifelong passion for the work of America's greatest architect. Since 2016, as the president and CEO of the Frank Lloyd Wright Foundation, he has stewarded Wright's legacy to help people discover and embrace Wright's architecture that connects us with nature, art, beauty, and each other. The **Frank Lloyd Wright Foundation** makes Wright's homes and studios at Taliesin (Wisconsin) and Taliesin West (Arizona) available to the public, to scholars and artists, and to design students through its programs, including the Taliesin Institute.

For Jorgen Ove Trulsson, without whom this would not have been possible.
—NBT

First published in the United States of America in 2024 by
RIZZOLI INTERNATIONAL PUBLICATIONS, INC.
300 Park Avenue South, New York, NY 10010
www.rizzoliusa.com

Publisher: Charles Miers
Editor: Douglas Curran
Production Manager: Alyn Evans
Managing Editor: Lynn Scrabis
Copy Editor: Victoria Brown
Proofreader: Sarah Stump

Designed by David Skolkin

Printed and bound in China

MIX
Paper | Supporting responsible forestry
FSC® C008047

2024 2025 2026 2027 2028 / 10 9 8 7 6 5 4 3 2 1

ISBN-13: 978-0-8478-3591-1
Library of Congress Control Number: 2024933943

Page 1: Frank Lloyd Wright, in the shadows of Taliesin West's Pergola.

Pages 2–3: Taliesin West's historic core, as viewed from the landscape of the Prow.

Page 4: The Pergola creates shadow patterns along the walkway next to the Drafting Studio.

Front cover: An iconic view of Taliesin West's historic core building, with steps leading up to the Drafting Studio on the left and the original dining room on the right.

Back cover: A current view of the Garden Room, designed originally as the Wrights' private living room.

Endpapers: Rendering of Taliesin West site ca. 1962, by Allen Lape "Davy" Davison, Vern Swaback, and Dan Novak, members of the Taliesin Fellowship.